THE LOCKHEED
CONSTELLATION

THE LOCKHEED CONSTELLATION

Ken Wixey

TEMPUS

First published 2001

PUBLISHED IN THE UNITED KINGDOM BY:

Tempus Publishing Ltd
The Mill, Brimscombe Port
Stroud, Gloucestershire GL5 2QG
www.tempus-publishing.com

PUBLISHED IN THE UNITED STATES OF AMERICA BY:

Arcadia Publishing Inc.
A division of Tempus Publishing Inc.
2 Cumberland Street
Charleston, SC 29401
(Tel: 1-888-313-2665)
www.arcadiapublishing.com

Tempus books are available in France and Germany
from the following addresses:

Tempus Publishing Group	Tempus Publishing Group
21 Avenue de la République	Gustav-Adolf Straße 3
37300 Joué-lès-Tours	99084 Erfurt
FRANCE	GERMANY

British Library Cataloguing in Publication Data.
A catalogue record for this book is available from the British Library.

ISBN 0 7524 1766 5

Typesetting and origination by Tempus Publishing.
PRINTED AND BOUND IN GREAT BRITAIN.

Contents

Acknowledgements

The author wishes to express his gratitude to the following companies and individuals without whose generous assistance this book would have remained just another project: The Lockheed California Co., for its exceptional help and advice, especially Robert C. Ferguson for the supply of many photographs; Shirley Lee (TWA); Peter Joel (Pan American World Airways); Ken Groves and John J. White (QANTAS); Christine Howarth (Lufthansa); Bob Harris (Air France); Rod Barlow (KLM); Lizzan Peppard (Aer Lingus); Martin Thompson (Northwest Orient); Guilherme Tully (VARIG SA); Jane Whigham (Air Canada) and the Public Relations Departments of Air India International, Eastern Air Lines and Swissair.

Gratitude is also expressed to Brian Stainer (Aviation Photo News) and Roger P. Wasley, for permission to use their photographs. Further assistance was rendered by Peter J. Marson and Air Britain, when certain valuable information was gleaned from their excellent, very detailed account of the Constellation family, published some years ago, a book recommended to anyone seeking individual Constellation construction numbers (cns), registrations and/or serials.

Introduction

The Lockheed Constellation, or 'Connie', as she became known, was probably the most aesthetically pleasing four-engine piston aeroplane to ever reach quantity production. It was a magnificent and extremely efficient aeroplane, deserving the many accolades bestowed upon it. It must surely rank among the all-time greats in aviation history.

On 9 January 1943 thousands of Lockheed employees lined the runways and hangars at Lockheed's Air Terminal to wait for the first Constellation to make its maiden flight. That aeroplane was the forerunner of a long line of commercial models and was the first modern transport of its kind, designed for high-altitude and over-the-weather flying. At that time the Constellation could carry the heaviest load and cover the longest distance in the shortest time, at the least cost, of any transport aeroplane flying.

That first Constellation was the result of meetings in mid-1939 between representatives of Transcontinental and Western Airlines (later Trans World Airlines) and Lockheed engineers. An aeroplane was visualized which would carry a 6,000lb payload a distance of 3,500 miles, with a crew of six, at a cruising speed of 250-300mph and an altitude of approximately 20,000ft. Initially conceived to have a take-off weight of 72,000lb and a maximum landing weight of 65,000lb, the new transport was progressively increased in landing weight to 67,000lb, then 70,000lb, while still in the design stages. Increases in permissible landing weight made corresponding increases in permissible take-off weight possible and, following Lockheed test flights, the prototype Constellation take-off weight was increased to 86,250lb and the landing weight to 75,000lb.

When it was originally introduced the Constellation was intended for civil use, but the Second World War was then some three years past and the United States Army Air Force (USAAF) grabbed the type for fast transport duties. They found it could exceed the speed of some versions of the Japanese Mitsubishi A6M Zero fighter. It was faster than any contemporary four-engine bomber and had the capability to airlift an armoured fighting vehicle non-stop over long distances.

After the war, development of the Constellation continued apace and several civil and military variants emerged, among them the 'stretched' Super Constellation. This was capable of flying non-stop, with full reserves, over a distance of 3,920 miles at long-range cruising speeds. This version incorporated enough power to take-off with a gross weight of 133,000lb from short runways, such as those found on small, mid-ocean islands. At sea level the Super Constellation Model 1049E could take-off with a gross weight of 133,000lb and clear a 50ft obstacle in 4,600ft.

Lockheed referred to their Super Constellation as the only true transatlantic aircraft by virtue of its ability to accomplish the task without the sacrifice of revenue-paying traffic on these long-range flights, even westbound against prevailing headwinds. By January 1953, Constellations had made more than 40,000 Atlantic crossings, a typical long-range flight being the New York to Paris run, a distance of 3,660 miles, flown at an even greater speed and with an even larger payload with Super Constellations.

The last in the commercial Constellation series was the Starliner, a greatly updated variant. Unfortunately, it was soon ousted from major airline service with the introduction of the new generations of jet airliners entering service. As these jetliners took over the major routes many Constellations, Super Constellations and Starliners were relegated to secondary duties, operating with less significant airlines. Quite a number ended up as freighters and became an asset to small operators, especially in Latin American countries. Other machines quickly became redundant and, sadly, fell before the breakers' torch. Before their demise, however, the Constellation family had carried many thousands of passengers comfortably, safely and speedily to destinations all over the world.

This then is the story of a classic aircraft type. It is the author's intention that this book be regarded as a tribute, in its small way, to the Lockheed Constellation in all its forms, civil and military. An aircraft considered as probably the most elegant and successful four-engine piston airliner ever produced in the United States.

1 Background History

The giant Lockheed Aircraft Corporation owed its origins to two brothers, Malcolm and Allan Loughead (pronounced Lockheed), of San Francisco. In 1913 they designed and built a floatplane, known as the Model G. This machine was employed for a number of years carrying passengers on pleasure flights in the area and, later, at Santa Barbara. It was here that the brothers founded the Loughead Aircraft Manufacturing Co.

By 1916 the brothers had taken on John K. Northrop as an aircraft designer. They intended to design and build a twin-engine flying boat for US Navy service but this did not materialize and, during the remaining years of the First World War, Loughead modified and constructed Curtiss flying boats under contract. After the war, the company tried to continue their aircraft business by producing a small sporting biplane but this venture fell through and the Loughead name temporarily vanished from the aviation scene.

During 1926 Allan Loughead and John Northrop formed the Lockheed Aircraft Company. Later John Northrop left Lockheed to start up on his own but not before he had left behind him the legacy of the well-known Vega high-wing monoplanes, one of which, called *Winnie Mae*, became famous in the 1930s when Wiley Post and Harold Gatty made their record-breaking round-the-world flights.

Gerald Vultee replaced Northrop at Lockheed and was responsible for creating a number of familiar Lockheed aircraft types, including the Altair and Orion. The Orion was, in fact, the first commercial production aircraft to incorporate a retractable landing gear and the first in its class to possess a top speed of over 200mph. The development of civil aviation during the 1930s owed much to the Orion, especially among smaller airlines. With its superb performance and relatively economical running costs this single-engine, low-wing monoplane helped to firmly establish a number of embryonic airlines. They included: CMA/Mexicana, Aerovias Centrales and Lineas Aereas Mineras SA (LAMSA), in Mexico; Bowen Airlines, in the US, and Swissair, in Europe.

Having established themselves as a successful manufacturer of civil aircraft, Lockheed decided to move to Burbank, California. However, with the 1930s depression Lockheed, which had become a division of the Detroit Aircraft Corporation (affiliated to the giant US automobile industry), found itself in financial difficulties. But, with the help of a fresh management team, which possessed a great knowledge of aviation and its contemporary requirements, the Lockheed Aircraft Co., as it became known, survived to embark on design and construction programmes for a new generation of twin-engine transport aircraft. These would include the Model 10A Electra, 12A, 14 Super Electra (from which evolved the famous military version, named the Hudson) and the Model 18 Lodestar. Additionally, there was to emerge the P-38 Lightning, a twin-boom, long-range, single-seat fighter.

The famous Lockheed Vega, NR-105-W Winnie Mae, *which made a round-the-world flight during June and July 1931.*

Obviously this scale of production demanded substantial amounts of both capital and working space and Lockheed realized that, for the level of production it anticipated, the facilities then available were inadequate. The company leased its property and, initially, the management were not keen to invest in modernizing plant and buildings which it did not own. However, late in 1936 the Lockheed board decided to purchase the land and buildings in order to facilitate aircraft production.

That important step involved what was to become the B-1 factory at Burbank, as well as some forty-three acres of land and around 108,000sq.ft of plant, requiring new capital to be raised. Added to this were the development costs of the latest Model 14 twin-engine transport. Efforts were made to substantially increase Lockheed's assets, which included two stock issues bringing in $1.6 million. Much of this was spent on new buildings and installing updated machinery and equipment. With a new administration centre and engineering office erected by 1938, production facilities had doubled and some 250,000sq.ft of floor space was available. At that time a large British order for Hudson reconnaissance bombers had been accepted. Lockheed's working capital was approximately $650,000, while there was actually $334,000 in the company's bank.

Several other aircraft manufacturers considered Lockheed's acceptance of the Hudson order for Britain's Royal Air Force (RAF) too much of a risk because of their limited facilities but the company president, Robert E. Gross, did not agree and was confident the contract could be fulfilled to the letter. In December 1938 Gross told his 2,500-strong workforce of his feelings about the British contract for 250 Hudsons, an order worth a possible $25million to the company and one which he was determined to complete on time. Then the vice-president of the California Bank, Charles A. Barker Junior, became vice-president of Lockheed, in charge of finance. Immediately he and Gross invaded the credit market, raising $1.25 million,

Lockheed Model 9B Orion of Swissair, which in May 1932 commenced a high-speed Zurich-Munich-Vienna service. The engine was a 575hp Wright Cyclone R-1820-E. The Orion was the first commercial production aircraft to feature retractable landing gear

supplemented by a $3 million stock issue early in 1939. Thus, the Lockheed Aircraft Corporation was destined to become a member of the big-league in manufacturing civil and military aircraft. The 250th Hudson was rolled out seven and a half weeks ahead of schedule, resulting in further contracts involving nearly 3,000 Hudsons.

Lockheed had been building the idea of a four-engine, passenger-carrying aircraft for some time prior to the conception of the Constellation. A design project known as the Model 44 Excalibur was put forward and enlarged upon, with a suggestion by Pan American Airways (PAA) that a pressurized version, carrying up to forty passengers, be considered. Revised in this form, it was envisaged the projected airliner would incorporate a nose wheel, weigh some 40,000lb gross, have a cruising speed of 250mph at 12,000ft and possess a range somewhat less than that of the contemporary Boeing 307 Stratoliner.

In June 1939 another airline, Transcontinental and Western Air (TWA), later Trans World Airlines, approached Lockheed with its requirements for an aircraft that would be a marked improvement on the Boeing 307, a type TWA were already involved with. A meeting was arranged between the financial head of TWA, Howard Hughes, its president, Jack Frye, Lockheed's president, Robert E. Gross and the company's engineering representatives, Hall L. Hibbard and Clarence L. 'Kelly' Johnson.

TWA desired an aircraft with longer range, faster speed and higher altitude capability than the Boeing 307 Stratoliner. The airline's proposal was for a design that cruised at between 250 and 300mph, could carry a 6,000lb payload at an altitude nearing 20,000ft, and accommodate a crew of six for flight deck and cabins. Lockheed's response was to consider their Project 44 design seriously and, although this could not be regarded as the actual progenitor for their Model 49 layout (known as Excalibur A, before being renamed Constellation), it did provide an excellent basis to work on.

The main problem to be solved concerned the size and type of engines to be installed, for calculations soon made it apparent that this type of aircraft required

In this 1929 aerial view of the Lockheed aircraft factory, several newly-built, high-wing Vega monoplanes are clearly visible.

a large capacity power-plant. These figures related to the efficiency of large aero-engines running at a low percentage of their power rating with a minimum amount of supercharging. In a smaller power-plant there was a weight saving factor of 1,385lb, although more complex supercharging was required, and they would be capable of the performance demanded but the weight-saving advantage was lost after the distance flown exceeded 755 miles. Therefore, as the range increased the advantage of larger engines became apparent. For example, as the more powerful engines carried additional payload it was calculated that, given a range of 2,500 miles, the effective payload would exceed 3,000lb. The use of larger engines also improved take-off capability, gave a larger safety margin, simpler power-plant installation, more reliability due to the use of low cruising power, and improved maximum performance.

Choice of a suitable engine for Lockheed's new design was fairly easy, as for some years Curtiss-Wright had been producing a successful series of air-cooled radial engines, including the Whirlwind and Cyclone. The latter had by then been developed into a double-row 18-cylinder affair, the Wright R-3350-745C18BAS-1 Cyclone 18. This produced 2,200hp for take-off, a cruise rating of 1,400hp at 14,000ft, and its fuel consumption figure was less than that of the earlier R-2600 Cyclone 14. Thus, Lockheed decided to power their new Model 49 design with four Cyclone 18s, an engine which, in its progressive forms, would be adopted as the standard power-plant for all models of the Constellation.

To minimize the drag effect of the four, big radials, a reverse-flow cowling design was considered and eventually produced. This underwent tests in one of six wind

Powered by two 400hp Pratt & Whitney SB2 Junior radials, this Lockheed 10A Electra is seen in 1934 serving with Northwest Airlines.

tunnel facilities, as did all major components of the Model 49. Most wind tunnel tests on the Constellation took place at the University of Washington and in the Lockheed Aerodynamic Laboratory. However, some tests were undertaken at the California Institute of Technology or with the National Advisory Committee for Aeronautics (NACA) with its three wind tunnels, one each for high-speed and spinning tests, and the third (a 19ft affair) for general testing.

In order that a proper engine installation was developed for the L-049, Lockheed produced a large-scale model nacelle incorporating a 30hp motor. This enabled the company to try out the reverse-flow cowling and a variety of standard-type cowlings. It was proved during a series of tests that the reverse-flow cowling idea was not particularly efficient. The incoming cooling air, passing backwards to the engine by induction via slots in the leading-edge of the wing, had to be exhausted behind the large propeller spinner, while the reversal of the airflow twice, through 180 degrees, contributed much to a substantial internal flow loss, which was not compensated for by the lower basic nacelle drag of the streamlined units. Despite other experiments being tried out, one of which involved blowers being built into the spinners, it was finally decided to adopt a standard type of straight-through cowling for the L-049 Constellation design.

The problem now facing Lockheed's engineers, led by Clarence L. 'Kelly' Johnson and Hall L. Hibbard, was the formulation of an optimum airframe in which these four, massive engines, by contemporary standards, could be installed. Their main objective was to be in accordance with the conception of a long-range, high-altitude, high-speed transport aircraft in which the basic requirement was a low operating cost. But the new design's flight characteristics had to possess a substantial improvement, compared with its contemporaries, and have maximum controllability available for both emergency and normal flight conditions.

A Lockheed 10A Electra early in the Second World War, serving with the Royal Air Force in standard camouflage for the period. Its serial number was W9106 and it flew on communications and training duties with the RAF.

The prototype Lockheed Model 12 was a scaled down 10A, seating six passengers. A total of 114 were produced as the Model 12A, powered by two, 400hp, Pratt & Whitney Wasp Junior SB2 engines. The first flight was on June 27 1936.

Seen here, during 1938-1939, is a Lockheed Model 14, G-AFGN, of British Airways, powered by a pair of 750hp, Pratt & Whitney Hornet radials.

A Lockheed Hudson Mk III reconnaissance bomber of the RAF, destined for Coastal Command service. It has already had its Boulton & Paul dorsal gun-turret fitted. Hudsons gave Lockheed their first big export order in 1938.

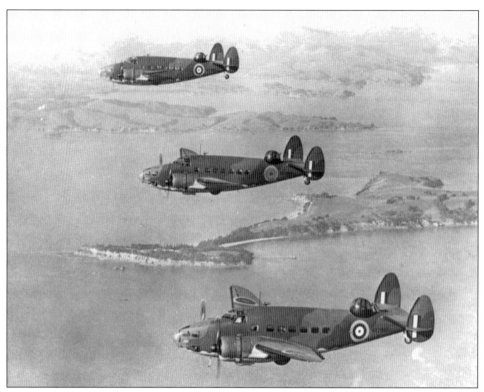

These Lockheed Hudson Mk IV bombers are with the Royal New Zealand Air Force. Serialled NZ 2001/02/03, they are part of a contract transferred from the RAF and/or Royal Australian Air Force, c.1940-41.

While the Lockheed 14 Super Electra provided an excellent basis for the Hudson bomber, its updated fourteen-seat version was the Model 18 Lodestar. This Lodestar (NC33664) is seen in 1938-39 with Pacific Alaska Airways, which was a subsidiary of Pan American Airways.

Lockheed owed much of its success to Robert E. Gross. As president of the company in 1938, he was responsible for securing the initial British contract for Hudson bombers for RAF service, thus providing Lockheed with a firm foundation on which to build its future programmes.

Charles A Barker, vice-president of Lockheed at the time of the first contract for Hudson bombers for the RAF. It was he and Robert E. Gross who managed to raise enough capital (Barker had been vice-president of the California Bank) to cover the British Hudson order.

From beneath a Hudson's port wing a long line of Hudson bombers await delivery at Burbank for delivery to the RAF. Notice the dorsal turrets are not fitted (Boulton & Paul gun turrets would be installed in the UK).

The wind tunnel at Lockheed's Aerodynamic Laboratory, Burbank works, California. Here a Model 1649 Starliner is being prepared for tests.

This fine portrait photograph is of the late Clarence L 'Kelly' Johnson, who was principally responsible for creating numerous Lockheed aircraft designs including the entire Constellation family.

2 Development Stages

It was planned that cabin pressurization, air refrigeration and air-conditioning would be incorporated into the L-049 layout. The type also had to conform with Amendment 56 of the Civil Air Regulations transport flight requirements regarding its ability to operate safely from small airfields. This meant it was essential that a high overall lift coefficient be obtained for the aircraft while carrying the heaviest possible load. The most effective flap for this purpose was Lockheed's Fowler-type, as used on their Model 14 and Hudson bomber, this resulting in a modified version of this flap being constructed and tested in the wind tunnel. However, when applied to the Constellation, these updated flaps created additional problems with the landing performance during tests, especially where elevator control and aileron control were concerned when two engines were inoperative on the same side.

Another problem arose in relation to rudder control, due to the large engines powering a relatively small airframe. Lockheed', having had considerable previous experience with twin fins and rudders, knew that when directional stability was less important than directional control, multiple vertical tail-surfaces held the advantage over a single unit. However, this was not the case in aeroplanes with far less power, when a single fin and rudder was preferred, mainly because of its lighter weight and less complicated structure. At the opposite end of the scale, Lockheed's L-049 was provided with triple fins and rudders, but slipstream effect from the four propellers necessitated the large horizontal tailplane being located on the upper rear fuselage, the camber line of which was raised. Thus, with two inset fins and rudders, and a third on the fuselage centreline, the L-049 would require little trim when its flaps and landing gear were lowered.

If minimum control speeds and other basic advantages were to be obtained, the next problem to be overcome on such a large aircraft as the Constellation would be the maximum controllability of all moveable flying surfaces. Although it had been already decided that incorporating hydraulic boosters for all controls was the most practical answer, it was not going to be easy. There would be extremely difficult technical problems to overcome, and certainly objections from official sources, due to complex mechanical devices being installed in substitution for the more familiar and reliable control-cable systems then prevalent on the majority of contemporary aircraft types. A compromise was reached, however, whereby the hydraulic booster system was complemented by a back-up emergency layout.

Lockheed was involved with developing hydraulic control surface boosters during 1939, prior to design work on the Constellation starting. A decision to incorporate this form of controllability in the L-049 was only finalized after a thorough investigation of all the factors involved. The findings concluded that the advantages of control surface boosters far outweighed the effects of earlier systems, but there were no existing values upon which to work in deciding what control forces pilots wanted on a large aircraft, so Lockheed manufactured a number of units containing variable boost ratios.

This resulted in a number of pilots undertaking a considerable amount of flying time on the project and eventually a set of figures was produced which could be used for the Constellation's control surface boosters. To obtain these results several critical control conditions were applied during the trials, one involving landing at the minimum control speed with two engines feathered, while other landing approaches were carried out in various turbulent air-conditions. These studies, made with suitable control loadings, resulted in some interesting basic requirement figures: with the elevator at full deflection the desirable force on the wheel was 50-80lb (maximum obtainable: 160lb); with the rudder at full deflection the desirable force on the pedal was 150lb (maximum obtainable: 500lb); with the aileron partially deflected the desirable force was 10ft/lb (maximum obtainable: 35ft/lb right and 30ft/lb left). Elevator forces down to 35lb were actually tried out in some landings, but proved too light. On the L-049 Constellation the desired forces were obtained with the exception of the ailerons, with which difficulties arose in attaining the required figure due to a 5-6ft/lb friction factor in the system.

It was certainly not a simple matter to achieve such results. This is perhaps better understood when it is realized the horizontal tailplane of the Constellation had an area 10sq.ft greater than the wing area of a Lockheed 10A Electra twin-engine transport, or nearly half that of a Douglas DC-3 wing. Obviously, a substantial boost ratio would be required to move a quarter of this area through a forty-degree arc, at an airspeed of 90mph, with a desired force of 80lb.

Such a large elevator was necessary on the Constellation due to the design requirements insisting on the type having the ability to operate from small airfields, a factor intended to allow larger payloads to be carried from more places. This demanded exceptionally good control where the elevator, rudder and

This photograph is of a Netherlands East Indies Air Force Lockheed Model 18 Lodestar (LT913) on finals. Here the lowered Fowler flaps and runners are clearly visible.

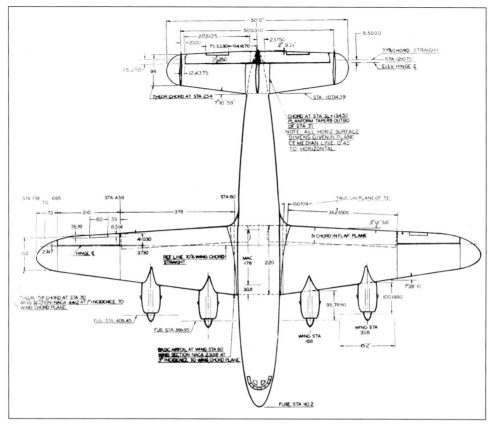

Planform drawing (photocopy Lockheed ex-works) of the original Model 49 (USAAF C-69). Note: width of tail plane = fifty feet.

ailerons had to operate under extremely difficult conditions. Also, with four such powerful engines, if one was feathered the rudder and aileron control problem was greater than that of other transport aircraft at a given airspeed. This was because of the distance between the fuselage and engines, as well as the necessarily large diameter propellers. Thus, in order to provide optimum landing characteristics, the incorporation of a powerful elevator was essential.

Final boost ratios for the L-049 Constellation proved to be much higher than those for other aircraft types, which normally worked out at around 3:1 or 4:1. In the Constellation's case the figures were: elevator 9.33:1, rudders 23:1, ailerons 26:1. These ratios were made practicable because a small amount of servo-action was used on trim tabs. This had no adverse effect on drag, area or weight factors.

The next stage in the L-049's development was the construction of a full-scale layout of the aircraft's hydraulic system, involving the boosters, landing gear, flaps, pumps, all pipework installation, automatic pilot, brakes and a cockpit mock-up. This was carried out in Lockheed's laboratory and everything was measured to take up the exact position it would fill on the actual aircraft. Four motors, built by the

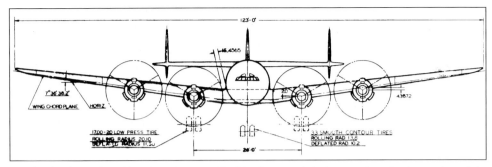

In this head-on view (drawing photocopy Lockheed ex-works) the complete circular section of the fuselage is apparent. Also the wing dihedral and again the massive proportions of the tail unit.

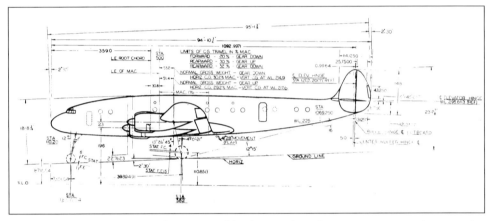

The side view drawing (again photocopy Lockheed ex-works), shows to some extent the serpentine appearance of the fuselage contours. The conventional style windscreen, despite a number of alternatives offered, was chosen to avoid structural problems relating to the cabin pressure systems.

Ford Motor Co., simulated the aero-engines. Operated from the cockpit, they provided impetus for the hydraulic pumps. Flaps and the landing gear were subjected to simulated air loads, while huge springs were used to create actual air load conditions on the elevators, rudders and ailerons. The load figures themselves resulted from wind tunnel tests and, to ensure that the differing speed ranges of the L-049 were tested under load conditions, a programme was set up to reproduce loadings expected to occur at 80, 120, 200 and 350mph. Another very stringent test involved freezing the entire empennage in a temperature of –70F, after which the controls were operated and the forces working on them were measured to study the hydraulic booster system at very low temperatures. A contamination test was also carried out, whereby dirt and water were deliberately added to the hydraulic fluid, following which the system was run at normal and low temperatures.

The aesthetic curves of the Constellation's fuselage were not incorporated just to provide the aircraft with an exceptionally fine configuration, but for more technical reasons. To begin with the large 15ft-diameter propellers necessitated an extremely

Wing section of the Lockheed P-38 Lightning twin-boom fighter was finally adapted for use in the Constellation transport. This P-38L Lightning is with the USAAF, serial 44-25419, and shows off to advantage the type's sleek lines and most importantly the wing profile.

long travel on the nose wheel leg, the length of which was designed to be reduced as much as possible by somewhat lowering the mean camber line of the fuselage at the forward section. Aft of the wing a limited downward curve was embodied to reduce drag at the maximum lift:drag ratio of the aircraft. In this way the fuselage possessed a profile something similar to the cruising speed airflow over the wing, a factor resulting in a small reduction in drag. It was also necessary to raise the fuselage camber line at the rear, in conjunction with the horizontal tailplane, to allow the triple vertical tail surfaces to be located in accordance with the required ground clearance.

Initially the flight deck windscreen was to have been incorporated within the fuselage contours, but mock-up tests showed this formula would be unsatisfactory, mainly due to poor visibility for the pilots and problems with pressurization associated with that form of structure. Consequently alternative windscreen designs followed, including a faired nose cockpit situated below the main floor level, a twin-cupola 'bug-eye' type, a single wide-type cupola, a more conventional 'Vee' type and, the design finally chosen, a single curved conical installation.

Accommodation for a flight engineer was included in the Constellation's flight deck layout. Despite the extra weight factor imposed by additional controls and instruments, it was decided this was compensated for with the gaining of optimum fuel consumption on long-haul flights. Also, a flight engineer provided a vital safety factor, by reducing the pilot's workload involving engine checks, electrical controls and cabin supercharging. Besides this, he would usually be more familiar with the aircraft's individual technical and maintenance history.

Various wing sections were tested for the Constellation design in the NACA's 19ft wind tunnel, these included laminar flow layouts as well as the more conventional

This one-off Lockheed XC-35 (36-353) ordered by the US Army, was the first 'civil' pressurized machine to fly in the USA. Powered by twin 550hp Pratt & Whitney turbocharged radial engines, it first flew May 7 1937, and paved the way for pressure systems employed in the Lockheed Constellation.

designs, for example, that used on Lockheed's P-38 twin-boom lightning fighter. Indeed the P-38 type of wing section was eventually chosen for, despite a drag penalty, this design incorporated high, maximum lift coefficients and superb stall characteristics. During the NACA tests the opportunity was taken to try-out the large chord de-icer boots of the pneumatic-pulse type. However, subsequent flight-testing proved this type to be unsatisfactory due to the disintegration of boot sections after a time in service. The result was a de-icing system developed for the Constellation but it was a number of years before the Constellation was fitted with a successful combined heating and pulsating system.

Major components of the L-049 were often tested to destruction at Lockheed's Research Laboratory, where one wing-joint fracture actually occurred and was later corrected. Flaps and other parts were subjected to remarkable life-tests under simulated load conditions, while a very important part of developing the L-049's structure was that of fatigue testing.

The first pressurized civil aeroplane to fly in the United States had been the Lockheed XC-35 Electra, and the company was able to use its experience with that earlier aircraft in developing a suitable pressure system for use in the L-049. This initially resulted in conditions whereby ground-level cabin pressure was retained up to an altitude of 9,000ft. In a similar manner, at 20,000ft altitude conditions were maintained as if at 8,000ft. A refrigeration unit was designed for the first system but not installed. The aircraft's pressure system was upheld by two engine-driven superchargers, which retained full cabin pressure independently.

Meanwhile the Civil Aeronautics Board (CAB) had produced findings after several years spent investigating the problems of fire prevention methods in aero-engines. Based on the CAB reports Lockheed installed a high level of fire prevention measures in the Constellation's engine compartments. In addition, the company made a study of electrical equipment installations relating to potential fire hazards, one result being the prevention of fire spreading from an engine nacelle by having the entire wing compartmentalized to provide proper ventilation, especially in the areas surrounding the fuel tanks.

Vibration tests were carried out on all main components of the L-049 and any possible flutter manifestation thoroughly investigated. A system of water ballasting was installed consisting of a central pumping station, an electric motor pump and large water tanks located at specific points in the fuselage together with the appropriate pipework. This system allowed Lockheed engineers to check on the Constellation's weight and centre of gravity shift when deliberately altered in flight. The cabin itself was loaded with water ballast by simply connecting a four-inch fire hose to the system and operating a valve.

Engine tests were carried out rigidly, with the fuel system operating under altitude and various temperature conditions, while to sort out any mechanical problems on the ground, extended running of the Wright engine was undertaken on a static test-bed, specially constructed for the purpose. Flight testing of the Wright R- 3350-745C18BA-1 Cyclone 18 radial engines, which were to power the L-049, was undertaken on a twin-engine Lockheed B-34 Ventura bomber a Lodestar development employed by Lockheed as a flying test-bed with similar performance figures to the Constellation. Nicknamed *Ventellation,* this aeroplane was later purchased by Curtiss Wright to further develop their R-3350-35 engines. On one particular test the time taken to completely change an engine on a Constellation was tried out and resulted in the remarkably fast time of twenty-seven and a half minutes.

Evolved from the Lodestar, the Lockheed Ventura was designed as a bomber. This particular aircraft, however, was used by Lockheed as a flying test-bed for the Wright R-3350-745C18BA-1 Cyclones which would power the Model 49 (USAAF C-69) Constellation. Nicknamed Ventellation *it later flew with Wright's as an engine test-bed.*

3 The Model 49 Prototype

In its original form, the Lockheed Constellation took some four years to design and develop, a period of time when numerous technical problems presented themselves. After construction of the first machine started in 1940, it became apparent that Lockheed's Model 49 was probably the most technically advanced transport aircraft in the world.

Of all-metal construction, the fuselage contained a circular cross-section and curved centre-line, which accentuated the longitudinal aerofoil effect with its lifting qualities. Up to fifty-five passengers could be accommodated with baggage. Access to the passenger compartment was via a door on the port side of the fuselage behind the wing trailing edge. A door located forward in the starboard fuselage side provided entry for the flight crew, while any cargo or large baggage was conveyed in a freight hold beneath the cabin floor. All cabin space was pressurized, allowing operations up to an altitude of 30,000ft. At 10,000ft sea level conditions could be maintained.

The all-metal wing structure was comprised of aluminium alloy with a smooth, stressed-skin, flush-riveted covering. The aerofoil sections were, in fact, scaled-up versions of the Lockheed P-38 Lightning fighter wing aerofoil section. Giant area-increasing Lockheed-Fowler type flaps were located along the wing trailing edges and, alongside them, were the fabric-covered, aluminium-alloy ailerons. The wings actually contained engine access passages in order that an engineer could attend a troublesome engine while airborne.

The tail unit, featuring the large, pear-drop shaped triple fins and rudders, was also an all-metal affair with metal covered fins and horizontal stabiliser. The rudders and elevators were fabric-covered. Trim tabs were incorporated in all these moveable components.

The Constellation featured a tricycle landing gear in which the two main units consisted of twin wheels mounted on a single, Lockheed, shock-absorbing strut. These main wheels fully retracted, in a forward and upward direction, into the inner engine nacelles, where they were completely enclosed by folding hinged doors. The nose wheel was distinguishable by its exceptionally long strut and was also fitted with dual wheels, the whole unit fully retracted backwards into a recess within the lower front fuselage, where it was enclosed by a pair of lengthy hinged doors. As a precaution against the possibility of a 'tail low' landing, a fully retractable skid was installed below the rear fuselage.

Four 2,200hp Wright R-3350-35 Cyclone, air-cooled radial engines, each driving a Hamilton Standard Hydromatic three-blade, metal, constant-speed, fully-feathering propeller, initially provided power for the Constellation. Prior to any official performance figures being released, it is interesting to observe that in 1943 estimates for the new transport were given to include an operating speed of 280mph at 25,000ft, a landing speed of 77mph and a range of 4,000 miles at operating speed. Later, after the military C-69 version had entered

Here the prototype C-69 Constellation (c/n 1961) is on a test-flight over California in early 1943. It has an olive drab military finish. Although initially civil-registered as NX25800, it became USAAF No 43-10309.

service with the USAAF, one report revealed that the transport had achieved a top speed of 329mph at 16,000ft.

The confidence of civil airlines in the Constellation had been apparent. Even before construction of the prototype began, in 1940, TWA placed an initial order for nine machines. PAA quickly followed this with a contract for forty of the transoceanic-type L-049s in June the same year, while TWA ordered a further thirty-one machines at the same time. However, world events soon drastically changed with the eruption of the Second World War. After the Japanese attack on Pearl Harbor brought the US into the conflict, the USAAF decided to invest in Lockheed's L-049 as a fast military transport. In the event TWA and PAA waived their rights to the first production batches of Constellations in favour of the USAAF, which ordered 180 L-049 Constellations designated as the military C-69.

The prototype Constellation was ready to undertake taxiing and pre-flight trials towards the end of 1942 but it was considered necessary to provide the pilot with some form of warning when critical stresses were imposed on the nose wheel's extremely long strut. Such stresses were most likely to occur during rapid turns or when there was an unbalanced application of the wheel-brakes or engine power. If this problem arose, an indication was passed to the pilot via micro-switches on the nose wheel structure, making a red warning-light glow in the cockpit.

A number of pre-flight tests were carried out on the prototype Model 49 (military C-69) before its first flight on 9 January 1943. The aircraft (cn.1961) was civil registered

Another angle on the C-69 Constellation prototype showing its contoured fuselage to advantage. Even in military drab finish this aircraft was aesthetically pleasing and full of great potential for future commercial use.

NX25800 but was finished in a military paint scheme of olive-drab upper-surfaces and grey under-surfaces. Classified as a USAAF machine, it was allotted the military serial number 43-10309. Five crew members boarded the prototype C-69 for its initial flight. These were test pilots Milo Burcham (Lockheed) and Edmund T. Allen (on hire from Boeing), research and design engineer Clarence L. 'Kelly' Johnson, as well as Rudy Thoren and Richard Stanton of Lockheed. As the new transport thundered away from Burbank it was cheered on its way by hundreds of Lockheed VIPs and employees who had taken up vantage points beside the runway and around the air-terminal hangars. Even in its drab war-paint the prototype C-69 was a grand sight as the four mighty Cyclone engines carried her elegant shape into the Californian skies for the first time. As a precaution, the landing gear was left in its lowered position. After circling the San Fernando Valley a few times the first of many C-69s headed north for the USAAF base at Muroc Dry Lake (now Edwards Air Force Base), where it landed after a flight lasting one hour. This initial flight went without incident. It was followed by a further five test flights out of Muroc, which went smoothly and proved successful, so much so that the formal test flight programme commenced almost immediately.

Failures of the hydraulic booster system were simulated in take-off and landing tests, while a number of rough-air tests were carried out under similar conditions. Normal take-off and landing behaviour was measured on a special grid and timer-camera device and this showed the relationship between wind tunnel and actual test flights to be reliable. During range tests it was found the prototype Constellation possessed a higher payload factor for its design range than was anticipated. For example, a single gallon (US) of fuel was used per mile at a cruising speed of 275mph on 52.5% power. Exhaustive tests were undertaken with the C-69's landing gear, one of which involved fitting small flaps to the tyres, thus causing the wheels to rotate, at a rate equal to 80% of the actual landing speed, prior to touchdown. This experiment reduced the tyre wear and landing shock considerably. Drag on the main landing gear wheels was reduced by 30% compared to a landing with no pre-rotation of the wheels. Another test involved deliberately forcing removal of one of the cabin windows while the fuselage was fully pressurized and contained a number of volunteer personnel. The loss of pressure caused little discomfort to either the crew or the 'guinea-pig' passengers. So, on 29 July 1943, the Lockheed C-69 prototype passed to the USAAF for its acceptance trials at Wright Field, Dayton, Ohio.

The first production C-69 Constellation (cn.1962) was the second machine built. Although intended for USAAF service, it emerged in the TWA colours: polished metal surfaces; red lettering on the fuselage; red, horizontal tail-stripes (two on each of the triple fins and rudders) and black letters and numerals on the wings. However, although civil in appearance, this second Constellation was allotted the USAAF serial number 310310 (43-10310), which it carried as black numerals between the red stripes on the outer fins and rudders.

The second C-69 Constellation prototype built for USAAF. It is in TWA livery but carries the military serial 310310 (43-10310) on its fins. This scheme was for promotional purposes only and for the record-breaking transcontinental flight across the USA in 1944, when the pilot was Howard Hughes.

TWA had in fact pre-arranged for the second Constellation to make a non-stop coast-to-coast promotional flight across the United States, piloted by Howard Hughes himself, with Jack Frye, the president of TWA, as co-pilot. The flight crew included flight engineer R.L. Proctor, navigator H. Bolton and wireless operator C.L. Glover. Also on board were Lockheed's Richard Stanton, R.J. Thoren and Thomas Watkins. VIP passengers on the flight included: S.J. Solomon, chairman of the Airline Committee dealing with post-war aviation policies; Lt-Col. C.A. Shoup, of the USAF; L.J. Chiappino; E.J. Minser; O.R. Olson; L. Sewell; L. Baron; R.L. Loomis and R. de Campo, of TWA.

The chosen route was from Burbank, to Washington DC, a distance of some 2,400 miles. Take-off was at 3.56 a.m. on 17 April 1944, when the second C-69 roared off into the dawn, heading east. Weather conditions were not too good for the flight, light icing was a constant problem and the C-69 had to alter course a number of times before resuming the planned route, flying at varied altitudes between 15,000ft and 18,000ft. When the Constellation landed, at Washington's National Airport, it had been airborne for six hours and fifty-eight minutes. This was the first of several records to be made by the type. The flight was followed by a period of official inspections, special flights and exhibitions, intended to impress military and civilian observers alike, after which 43-10310 was handed over to the USAF to serve in its official capacity as a high-speed military transport.

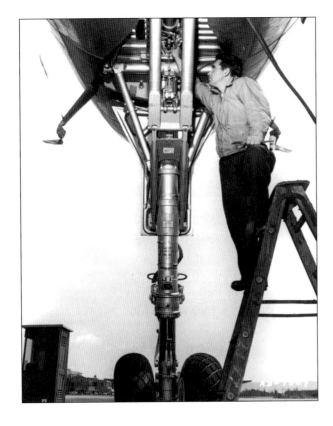

A Lockheed engineer checks the nose-wheel mechanism on an early L-049 Constellation. Note the exceptional length of this unit.

*Here the first production
Constellation has received its
full USAAF colour scheme of
overall natural metal.*

The US Army were more than pleased with the C-69. As well as the excellent fuel consumption figures attained, design performance had been achieved comfortably with a top speed of 347mph and a cruising speed of 275mph. The commodious fuselage of the military-type Constellation could accommodate up to sixty-four fully-armed troops. Alternatively, it was capable of carrying a light tank or other medium-sized military vehicles.

23 January 1945 saw TWA's Intercontinental Division being contracted to introduce the C-69 into the USAF Air Transport Command (ATC) service. During this period some significant, long-distance flights were carried out. For example, on 4 August 1945 a C-69C (42-945500) flew from New York to Paris in fourteen hours and twelve minutes, setting a new record time. This particular aeroplane (cn.1971) was the only C-69C model produced. It was in a VIP configuration, fitted to carry forty-three passengers. After the war this Constellation was sold to the civil market as NX54212 but, despite interest being shown in a further forty-nine of these VIP machines being produced as a civil type, no contract ever materialized. In the meantime, on 22 September 1945, another C-69 in USAF, ATC service covered the distance of 2,750 miles from Stephenville, Newfoundland, to Paris, in a record time of nine hours and twenty-two minutes.

A total of twenty-two Lockheed C-69 Constellations were scheduled for USAF service when VJ Day heralded the end of the Second World War. At that time, fifteen C-69s had been delivered, including the prototype, with a further seven practically ready for military service. These consisted of the original nine ex-TWA

This was the Republic XR-12, a four engine reconnaissance-bomber which was the basis for the RC-2 Rainbow forty-six seat passenger transport designed for Pan American Airways. Had it been available some 18 months beforehand, the Rainbow would have been a serious threat to Lockheed's Constellation.

machines taken over by the USAF and thirteen from the military contract for 180 C-69s signed in 1942. This order was later reduced to seventy-three C-69 strategic transports, which left Lockheed with a cancellation order on fifty-one aircraft. A decision had to be made whether to commence the design and development of a new version of the Constellation, or to convert the existing C-69 airframes into civil airliners. The result was a temporary, five-day closure of the Burbank plant as top-level meetings were held between Lockheed representatives. The decision was taken to proceed with a modification programme to convert the existing C-69s for commercial use and to produce a proper civil variant for civil airline use. This plan propelled Lockheed along the road to a great success story and secured the company's future in America's aircraft industry.

Initially, there was a considerable quantity of Government tooling available, as well as numerous components, constructional materials and a number of partially-completed C-69s ready for conversion into the planned airliner. A more important factor was saving the jobs of 15,000 Lockheed employees. The company saved enough time to be able to present their updated C-69 to the civil market, as the L-049, eighteen months in advance of the Douglas DC-6, Boeing Stratocruiser and Republic Rainbow. Within a fortnight of V J-Day Lockheed had an order backlog for 103 Constellations, with contracts signed by eight airlines, amounting to an order book value of $75.5 million.

The US Civil Aeronautics Board Approved Type Certificate No.763 was awarded to the Lockheed L-049 on 11 December 1945, after only twenty-seven hours of performance flight-testing. Meanwhile, the US War Assets Administration (USWAA) sold the USAF Constellations for civil use and, after refurbishing by Lockheed, nineteen passed into airline service. Unfortunately, two of the military C-69s were destroyed: one (cn.1972), 42-94551, in a fire at Topeka on 18 September 1945; the other machine (cn.1973), 42-94552, during structural tests at Wright Field. As for the prototype C-69, NX25800/43-10309, or *Old 1961* as she was sometimes

A nice aerial view of PAA's L-049 Constellation, NC88832, Clipper Flora Temple, *in original, all-metal, Pan American finish.*

known (after the cn.1961), it was updated, having four, Pratt & Whitney R-2800 radials installed, and designated the XC-69E. The aircraft was then offered for sale by the USWAA and purchased by Howard Hughes, but he appears to have done little with the aeroplane before selling it back to Lockheed in 1950.

An intensive modification programme was then started on *Old 1961*, the most obvious change being the 'stretched' fuselage, which provided a greater payload and a total cabin length of 56ft. These improvements were obtained by incorporating two new fuselage sections, 10ft 9in and 7ft 8in respectively, forward and behind the wing. Power was increased by installing four 2,700hp Wright R-3350-CA1 Cyclones. Porthole-style passenger windows were replaced by round-cornered square windows. Structural strengthening of the airframe was undertaken. Improvements were made to the pressurization and air-conditioning due to the larger fuselage. Cabin heating and cooling facilities were enlarged upon and the fuel tank capacity was increased to 6,550 gallons (US).

In this configuration *Old 1961* became the prototype Lockheed L-1049 Super Constellation, its civil registration being altered from NX25800 to NX67900. In her ensuing career this original Constellation flew as a test-bed for the radar systems under development for the Lockheed WV-2 (US Navy, radar picket aeroplane) and was fitted with auxiliary fuel tanks at the wing tips. Probably the most notable achievement of this particular aeroplane was as a test-bed for the 3,250ehp, Allison T-56 turboprop engine, one of which was located in the outer starboard position. Success of these trials on NX67900 resulted in that power-plant being chosen as the standard engine for the famous Lockheed C-130 Hercules transport.

Although this resplendent prototype for the L-1049 Super Constellation looks new, it is in fact the original prototype C-69 (old 1961) with lengthened fuselage, revised cabin windows, extra fuel capacity, uprated Cyclone 18 radial engines of 2,700hp each, wingtip tanks (not then standard on civil Constellations) and, of course, a rather splendid paint scheme.

Later old 1961 was used as a flying test-bed for 3,250ehp Allison T-56 turboprop engines. This proved so successful the T-56 was adopted as power for the then new Lockheed C-130 Hercules transport, the prototype of which (53-3397) is seen here as a YC-130A with four Allison T-56-A-ls.

4 The L-049/649/749 Series

Nineteen USAF C-69s became available for the civil market, the majority being acquired by TWA and British Overseas Airways Corporation (BOAC). Because of their previous allegiance to Lockheed's Constellation, TWA were afforded priority delivery of refurbished ex-USAF Constellations and the newly-built L-049 models as they came off the production line ready for commercial use. Indeed, TWA had purchased the last two surplus USAF C-69s, completed at Burbank in December 1945, these being cns 2021 and 2022 (ex-42-94560 and 42-94561), which became, respectively, TWA's N86500, *Star of the Mediterranean*, and N86501, *Star of the Persian Gulf*.

The next airline to receive new L-049s was PAA, which had earlier flown a C-69 (cn.1963), 43-10311, under USAF contract. PAA took an initial delivery of twenty-nine L-049 Constellations. On 19 January 1946 one of these flew 3,425 miles from New York, to Lisbon, Portugal, in nine hours and fifty-eight minutes, at an average speed of 344mph. On 3 February 1946 PAA inaugurated its Constellation service between New York and Bermuda. Eight days later the 3,450 miles between New York and Hum Airport, near Bournemouth, Hampshire, (the transatlantic terminal at that time), was covered by another PAA Constellation in twelve hours and six minutes, at an average speed of 285mph. This was the start of a regular service 'across the pond'.

On December 3 1945 a TWA L-049 (cn.2026), N86505, had been named *Paris Sky Chief* in a ceremony at Washington's national airport, before leaving for Paris, flying via Gander, Newfoundland, and Shannon, Eire, on an official proving flight. This machine was unfortunately lost, just over a year later, on 28 December 1946, at Rineanna, Eire.

Meanwhile, on 4 February 1946, TWA's Jack Frye had piloted another Constellation on a record breaking, non-stop flight from Burbank to New York, in seven hours and twenty-eight minutes. The following day TWA inaugurated its service from the US to France when L-049 Constellation (cn.2035), N86511, *Star of Paris*, left La Guardia Airport, New York, heading for Paris, piloted by Capt. Harold F. Blackburn. The flight took just nineteen hours and forty-six minutes. Ten days later, on 15 February, TWA commenced its New York to Los Angeles service, with an L-049 piloted by Howard Hughes. That flight took eight hours and thirty-eight minutes.

Some problems occurred with the L-049 in the early days of its airline service, mainly with engine auxiliary systems. A more serious setback took place on 11 July 1946 when TWA's N86513 (cn.2040), *Star of Lisbon*, was on a routine company training-flight. After some twenty minutes in the air the forward section of the aeroplane filled with smoke. The crew were unable to carry out an emergency landing and the Constellation crashed at Reading, Pennsylvania. Of the six persons on board, only one survived, having suffered serious injuries. Crash investigators found the fire had been caused by an electrical short-circuit which had ignited part of the cabin insulation. At the enquiry it was suggested that if an emergency hatch in the passenger

Here a TWA L-749 Constellation, N6008C, stands waiting its next flight at the developing London Heathrow during the 1960s.

An L-049 Constellation, NC86503, of TWA. This was one of the first civil production aircraft delivered to TWA, which flew its first Washington to Paris Constellation service on 6 February 1946.

London Airport (Heathrow), where PanAm L-049 Constellation, N88831 Clipper London, *has just landed in 1946 to become the first scheduled transatlantic service to use the airport.*

TWA began a Constellation service from Chicago to Cairo, Egypt, via New York and European cities on 3 May 1946. This rare shot shows a TWA L-049 Constellation flying past the Pyramids of Gizeh.

The 'office', flight deck of a Lockheed Model L 049 Constellation in which a flight engineer was employed to lighten the workload on the captain and first officer. Note the prominence of the throttle quadrant in the centre of the picture.

Lockheed Constellations were the first land-based aircraft to fly scheduled passenger services between the USA and Europe. TWA began its services across the 'pond' on February 5 1946. Here a TWA hostess prepares to serve dinner aboard a Constellation in 1946.

American Airlines was another Constellation operator and here one of their L-049s provides an impressive backdrop to its crew and full complement of passengers.

cabin had been opened, the smoke-filled area would probably have cleared. In any case, this accident meant a six-week grounding for Constellations while ninety-five modifications and improvements were carried out on the type. These included electrical systems, fireproofing (this applied to all civil aeroplanes as an improved standard) and replacement of the engine's fuel-injection method by carburettors.

The basic version of the L-049 was improved upon through six updates. The original L-049 was, of course, the civilianized C-69, with a maximum take-off weight of 86,250lb. The L-049A incorporated front wing-spar and main landing gear side-strut reinforcements. This was followed by the L-049B, which contained fuselage-detail modifications and new metering pins for the main landing gear units. Next came the L-049C, featuring a main landing gear strut-damper and a 15:1 elevator boost ratio, while the following L-049D had its inner wing sections reinforced. With the introduction of the L-149 and its fuel tanks in the outer wing panels, the gross take-off weight had risen to 100,000lb and four 2,200hp Wright R-3350-7455C 18BA3 Cyclones provided the power.

Mainly in response to Eastern Air Lines (EAL) requirements for a medium-range version of the Constellation, work commenced on a revised version of the type at Burbank, in May 1945. By then, a revised version of the Wright Cyclone power-plant was available, the R-3350-749C 18BD1, rated at 2,500hp. This engine was chosen to power the much updated L-649 Constellation. Making its first flight on 19 October 1946, the prototype L-649, N101 A, featured a number of design improvements, including revised engine cowlings, improved air-conditioning, more luxurious cabin furnishings and the installation of shock-mounted walling. Accomodation in the new model allowed for between forty-eight and sixty-four passengers as standard or, for high-density arrangements, eighty-one seats could be made available. There was 434 cu.ft of cargo space, extra fuel tanks were installed and the four, uprated Cyclones gave the L-649 a cruising speed of some 285mph. An innovation to this version was the 'speedpack', a special freight pannier, fitted ventrally beneath the centre fuselage. This pack gave the Constellation an additional 395 cu.ft of cargo space, enough for up to 8,300lb of cargo. It was ideal for use with machines on short-haul routes or where passenger density was low. One airline using speedpacks on its Constellations

These passengers aboard a TWA L-049 Constellation in the late 1940s would have been among the first to travel to Europe by air – a journey of some twenty hours from the United States East Coast. Note the pillows and blankets in the overhead racks to add extra comfort on night flights.

Shown in this excellent air-to-air shot is Pan American Airways L-049 Constellation, N88861, Clipper Winged Arrow, shortly after Pan Am introduced its white upper fuselage paint scheme.

With a more luxurious cabin finish and uprated Wright Cyclone engines, the Lockheed model L-649 was known as the 'Gold Plate Connie'. The L-649 shown here is NC 102A of Eastern Air Lines (The Great Silver Fleet) and is flying over the Rickenbacker Causeway. This particular machine was later updated to L-749A standard.

was Royal Air Maroc. The L-649 had a maximum take-off weight of 94,000lb but this increased to 98,000lb with the Model L-649A, which was, basically, the L-649 with fuselage and inner-wing reinforcements, as well as modified brakes. EAL purchased fourteen of the L-649As for $650,000 each. The air-conditioning and soundproofing turned out to be so good that the type was dubbed the 'Gold Plate Connie'. Entering service with EAL in May 1947, the L-649As began operating the company's New York to Miami, Florida, route the following month.

Even before EAL's L-649As had been delivered, Lockheed's design team was engaged in updating the Constellation layout. This was in response to the international growth of air travel in 1947 and the demand by airlines for aeroplanes with longer range and higher take-off capacity. The revised Constellation was designated L-749 and featured integral fuel tanks located within the outer wing sections. Each of these tanks had a capacity of 565 gallons (US), which added a further 1,000 miles to the aeroplane's range, thus enabling the 3,660-mile flight between New York and Paris to be made non-stop. Strengthened landing gear was installed in the L-749 and the maximum take-off weight had risen to 102,000lb. This was not detrimental to the payload, which remained the same as the earlier version. Power was still provided by four 2,500hp Wright R-3350-BD1 radials, giving a top speed of 350mph and a cruising speed of 328mph. Some L-649s were later modified to L-749 standard. The L-749 could also convey the underbelly speedpack, sometimes used on the L-649. This method of carrying small, freight loads, in addition to passengers, on short to medium-haul routes, proved a great asset. The

Interior cabin arrangement for the L-649, first Constellation built from the outset as a commercial type (earlier machines were military C-69 updates).

A good close-up at Heathrow in the early 1950s of the Wright GR-3350-749C 18BD-1 Cyclone radials, which powered this Lockheed 749 of Air India International. Air India's three L-749 Constellations at the time were VT-CQS (c/n 2504), VT-CQR (c/n 2505) and VT-CQP (c/n 2506).

speedpack was easily accessible, having an electronic hoist fitted for raising and lowering, while ground handling was facilitated by small wheels inset at each end.

The first orders for the L-749 came from Air France, with an order for fourteen machines, the first of which was delivered on 18 April 1947. In the US, PAA employed the first production L-749 on a round-the-world flight, starting from New York, on 17 June 1947. The route taken was via Gander, Shannon, London, Istanbul, Karachi, Calcutta, Bangkok, Shanghai, Tokyo, Manila, Guam, Wake Island, Midway, Honolulu, San Francisco and back across the US, to New York, where the L-749 landed on 1 July.

To fulfil a BOAC requirement for a Medium Range Empire (MRE) civil transport, early in 1947 it was proposed that a licence-built version of the Lockheed L-749 Constellation be produced in Great Britain by the Bristol Aeroplane Co. Ltd at Filton, Bristol. This projected Constellation would be powered by four Bristol Centauras 652 radial engines and, once the aeroplane had been suitably 'anglicised', should prove very beneficial to BOAC. However, this proposed offshoot of the L-749 never came to fruition, as the MRE idea ended up with the development of Bristol's own turboprop-powered Britannia design.

The L-749 was itself modified, to obtain a higher gross take-off weight and an additional 4,850lb payload. The fuselage, inner wing sections and landing gear were strengthened, while, at the same time, improvements were carried out on the braking system. These updates resulted in the L-749A, with a maximum take-off weight of 107,000lb. This version also had the capability to carry the speedpack, ventral, cargo pod fitted to the previous two models.

To complement its original Constellation fleet of L-049 and L-749s, Air France purchased ten of the L-749As. Four L-749As were ordered by South African Airways (SAA), the first machine, (cn.2623) ZS-DBR, was delivered on 24 April 1950. These were the first pressurized airliners to enter service with SAA. They replaced Douglas DC-4s on the Johannesburg to London route, known as Springbok, which flew via Nairobi, Khartoum and Castel Benito. Not only did the Constellations prove far superior in terms of comfort, they also reduced the flying time on this route to twenty-eight hours. Three years after the L-749As entered SAA service an interesting, though somewhat tragic, sequel arose. SAA had moved to its new International Air Terminal at Jan Smuts Airport, which opened on 3 October 1953. Subsequently, they introduced a jet service, using the ill-fated DH Comet 1. The Constellations were relegated to operating the Springbok route's tourist-class service, with seating arrangements for fifty-eight passengers. There then followed the tragic Comet 1 disasters at Calcutta, and off Elba and Stromboli. These led to the inevitable withdrawal of DH Comet 1 s from airline services. This resulted in SAA reverting to the L-749A Constellations on its first-class service, although the tourist-class passengers were still well-catered for, as by that time, there were five Springbok services operating weekly. Thus Constellations became SAA fleet flagships for a second time but, by 1958, they had been superseded by Douglas DC-7Bs, a type which reduced the total flying time for the journey to twenty hours. The Constellations continued to operate on SAA domestic routes until January 1959, flying services between Rhodesia (Zimbabwe) and South Africa.

Allotted to TWA as NC91207 (Fleet No 707), this Model 749 Constellation was in natural metal finish, this version being a modified L-649 with extra fuel tankage, strengthened landing gear and later leading to the L-749A.

Compare this flight deck interior of a Lockheed 749 with that of the earlier L-049 and the more sophisticated layout and improvements are apparent. Notice the fuel jettison valves installed in the cockpit roof.

A Lockheed L-749A in its element. This aircraft is seen in the 1960s as ZS-DBR of South African Airways (SAA) and wears a very smart finish.

Lockheed 749A Constellations were eventually ousted from the SAA Johannesburg to London 'Springbok' service in 1958 by the Douglas DC-7B, which reduced the total flying time for this route to twenty hours. Here a DC-7B of Eastern Air Lines flies along an American coastline.

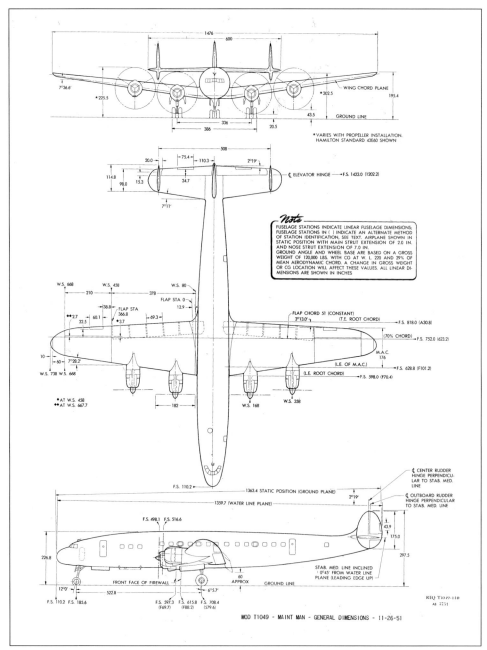

This photocopy of a Lockheed works drawing shows the layout in planform of the L-1049 Super Constellation to be powered by 2,800hp Wright R-3350-956-C 18CB1 engines. Note the increase in fuselage length.

5 A Super Constellation

Although a large number of reliable and mostly economical transport aeroplanes were in service with the world's airlines by the end of the 1940s, there was a growing demand for passenger-carrying types capable of flying the long-haul routes non-stop. At that time the greatest needs were among companies operating transatlantic and US coast-to-coast services, although there was a rising demand for more advanced types of aeroplanes on the transpacific routes. Competition was rife among airlines flying the US transcontinental services and a situation arose whereby the two great rival aeroplane manufacturers, Douglas and Lockheed, turned to revising their already proven designs in the forms of the DC-4 and L-749A respectively.

As previously mentioned, the Lockheed team converted the original C-69 prototype (cn.1961) into a 'stretched' version of the Constellation which, as NX67900, became prototype for the L-1049 Super Constellation. As such, this aeroplane made its initial flight on 13 October 1950, with test pilots J. White and R. Meskimen at the controls.

With greater economies and higher payloads in mind, Lockheed's designers had made a close study of the requirements of contemporary airlines. They were especially aware of the potential for a substantial growth in high-density passenger traffic over long-range international routes, factors which would require greater passenger capacity and more powerful engines. The Wright R-3350-956C 18CB-1, rated at 2,700hp, was initially available for the Super Constellation, while the insertion of an extra 18ft 4in of fuselage length allowed an increase in seating to sixty-nine first-class, or ninety-two tourist-class passengers. A first-class, transcontinental, sleeper version was available, with eight berths and up to fifty-five first-class seats.

The transition from the L-749A to the L-1049 Super Constellation configuration proved a complex procedure, involving more than 550 design changes, of which 360 were maintenance items. Hydraulic pressure throughout the Super Constellation under normal operating conditions was 1,700lb per sq.in. Power for this system was provided by four, engine-driven, Vickers hydraulic pumps. Power for emergency operation of the brakes and landing gear extension was produced by a Bendix hand-pump, while separate, electrically-driven, Pesco hydraulic pumps, one each for auxiliary rudder and elevator booster systems, were installed.

Lockheed studied the advantages for pilots of hydraulic power boost on the Constellation and L-1049 Super Constellation series. Hydraulic power-boosted surface control provided ease of operation and reduced pilot fatigue. With power boost, human control effort, multiplied by mechanical devices, resulted in minimum physical effort being required to fly the larger four-engine aeroplane. While power boost eliminated the heavy work of flying a large aeroplane, the pilot still had the 'feel' of control over his machine. In a five-year research programme, which brought the system to perfection, Lockheed engineers investigated the stick force (without boost) required by the aeroplane itself under critical conditions. They then determined the amount of muscular effort deemed most desirable by the pilots themselves.

In the design of the landing gear for the L-1049 Super Constellation, (the nose wheel leg of which was 9ft 6in long) hydraulic braking was provided completely in duplicate as a safety measure. This was complemented by reverse-pitch propellers where runway length was limited. Another safety feature was included; each wheel in the main twin-wheel units was able to support the full landing gear strut load when taking off or landing. The nose landing gear was steerable to fifty-nine degrees each side of centre, greatly improving the ground-handling qualities for of a Super Constellation. The tyres were 17in by 20in on the main wheels, and 33in on the nose wheels.

Wing design for the L1049 Super Constellation was essentially unchanged but, although aerodynamically identical to the earlier series, it incorporated integrally stiffened skinning on both upper and lower surfaces. This gave a lighter wing structure, reduced production costs and improved fuel tank capacity within the wings. This updated process was made possible by Lockheed's pioneering attitude to manufacturing techniques, whereby machines, greater and more powerful than any then previously used in aeroplane construction, were capable of forming massive pieces of aluminium alloy into the required shape for a specific aeroplane component. This made it possible to construct huge wing-panels, up to 45ft long, in one piece, so that the outer skin and strong, inner structure resulted in a single, lightweight unit.

This style of aeroplane manufacture took place in what was known, at Lockheed, as 'the Hall of Giants'. The company's employees were confident that their new equipment symbolized a new era in aeroplane construction techniques. To those at Lockheed it was the end of the 'bits and pieces' method. Now a 3,200lb chunk of tough aluminium alloy, 32ft in length, could be milled with great precision until only 800lb remained. Those pieces gouged out were salvageable and, in some cases, weighed more than Charles Lindbergh's Ryan monoplane, *Spirit of St Louis*, when empty. The single component made with this type of machining process for the Super Constellation was much stronger and lighter than the old types of panel, which had required 1,500 separate parts and 5,000 rivets.

The Constellation airframe could be redesigned with weight reduction as the primary motive while, at the same time, modification to the structure resulting in superior strength was now a viable proposition. This was thanks to Lockheed's own philosophy of avoiding undue weight penalties by taking advantage of previously unused margins of structural strength, which allowed exceptional increases in maximum weight with a minimum of modification. Thus, elongation of the fuselage, to 113ft 7in for the Super Constellation, was achieved with sound weight-economics in mind. There was a 40% payload increase, but the tare weight (minus fuel, crew and operating service material) was up by only 8,800lb. A further eight standard seats, or ten touring-class seats, could be accommodated in the additional cabin space made available by the lengthened fuselage, this ensured airline operators of increased profitability when they used Super Constellations. Lockheed's sales team had, in fact, worked out a formula covering this factor. They emphasized that, given an average flying time per aeroplane, per year, of 2,930 hours, and an average cruising speed of 280mph over a distance of 817,000 miles, using the extra eight standard seats, the extra annual profit would amount to $366,284.80.

The 'Hall of Giants' at Lockheed's Burbank works in the 1950s, where a batch of L-1049 Super Constellations is under construction.

Determined that Super constellation passengers would experience the utmost in comfort and convenience, Lockheed developed and produced, what must then have been, the most luxurious interior designed for any large capacity passenger aeroplane. They invested $1,500,000 and some 120,000 man-hours in it, with priority being given to compartmentalizing the fuselage so that considerable privacy could be enjoyed by passengers. Materials used included real leather, rich fabrics and natural woods. A club lounge was provided, in which special lighting effects and restful colour schemes were complemented by artistic murals and styles of interior decor which provided passengers with a sense of security, tranquillity and spaciousness. The latter factor was enhanced by the installation of 16 $\frac{1}{8}$in x 18 $\frac{1}{8}$in, square round-cornered, panoramic windows, which provided an increase of 85% in visibility over earlier porthole-type windows. These new windows featured double panes made from tough, non-crazing plastic, designed to withstand full cabin-pressure differential at maximum altitude. A circulation of warm air passed between the double safety panes, preventing misting and frosting up of the windows. The windows were tinted to obviate altitude glare and installed in such a way that they were not subjected to any structural load of the fuselage. Thirty-four large windows were fitted outboard to each row of passenger and relief-crew seats. Nine of these were mounted in separate emergency-exit panels, for the use of passengers. Two passenger entrance doors were provided, allowing the simultaneous loading and unloading of fare-paying passengers, while a separate door gave exclusive entrance and exit for the crew. The interior of the L-1049 also lent itself to flexibility for the airline operator, with quick conversion from one class to another (first-class to tourist-class, for example) being possible, or mixed classes could be accommodated.

The Super Constellation was, like its predecessors, fully pressurized, with sea level conditions prevailing at 12,300ft. Cabin pressure was maintained at a 5,000ft level when the aeroplane was cruising at 20,000ft and pressure was at an equivalent to 8,000ft when the altitude was 25,000ft. The pressurization equipment, produced and supplied by AiResearch, provided a 5.46lb per sq.in pressure, maintained by a pair of engine-drive superchargers, each capable of individually upholding full cabin pressure.

The L-1049 Super Constellation contained what was termed as a 'cabin within a cabin'. This meant the walling and ceilings of the passenger compartment were supported, inside the outer fuselage, by isolation-type mountings. Warm air was circulated within the resulting cavity and maintained the cabin temperature at a steady 75°F, even if the outside temperature measured -60°F. This system resulted from the installation of two, 125,000BTU per hour, internal combustion heaters.

At the other end of the scale, an important requirement for aeroplanes flying in tropical conditions was cabin refrigeration. On the Super Constellation, even where the outside temperature exceeded 100°F, the cabin was designed to retain an inner temperature of 70°F or so. Each passenger was provided with an individual air outlet, and 140lb of fresh air per minute could be introduced into the cabin. It was estimated that the cooling system was equal to running 320 domestic refrigerators, at a sixteen-ton refrigeration capacity. An interesting figure – it has been calculated that it requires one ton of refrigeration to freeze an equal amount of water in twenty-four hours.

As the Super Constellation was to operate on both transcontinental and intercontinental non-stop routes, Lockheed's design team realized the importance of providing maximum comfort and convenience for the crew. Engine noise was kept to a minimum, which helped facilitate communication between members of the crew considerably, alleviating reliance on the intercommunications system. A spare berth was provided in the forward compartment on the transatlantic version, for members of the crew, and, like the passengers, the captain and his crew enjoyed the comforts of the specialized heating and cooling systems. The L-1049's flight deck had more headroom than that of earlier Constellations. The controls and indicators were designed and located to provide the crew with easy access. To facilitate instrument reading at night, red panel lighting was installed, while an emergency lighting system was connected directly to the batteries, for use when the electrical system was disconnected.

A redesigned, laminated, electrically-heated windscreen, which provided the captain and flight deck crew with 21% extra visibility, became standard on the Super Constellation. This windscreen consisted of seven flat panels located 3.5in higher than those employed on earlier Constellation models. It was produced in impact-resistant units, as protection against what has become commonly known as a bird strike. These panels were specially designed to prevent the windscreen from icing over on the outside and misting up on the inside. This was accomplished by a layer of transparent, conductive coating called Nesa (non-electrostatic formulation A), applied as a heating element. The Nesa was operated by a power input of between 1kW and 4kW, and was

This Model L-1049 Super Constellation, N6201C, first flew in August 1951. It became the first Super Constellation to enter service with EAL, on 15 December that year, with the fleet number 201. Eastem used 14 Super Constellations on their New York to Miami service.

sprayed on 45 millionths of an inch thick on the inner surface of the outer panel of glass. The centre layer was a $\frac{1}{4}$in panel of elastic vinyl and inside, a $\frac{3}{8}$in panel of glass.

As a result of problems with wing de-icers on the earlier Lockheed Constellations, an improved design of de-icer boot was developed which did not fragment at speed. Manufactured by Goodrich, these new boots were operated by two pumps supplying high-pressure air to them. Two additional pumps were installed to act as back-up or emergency units. Consisting of a number of small, high-pressure tubes, made from tough, weather-resistant, synthetic rubber, each of the de-icer boot units was fitted into the leading edges of the wings, fins and horizontal tailplane. These boots were as tough as the aeroplane's structure itself, forming a smooth, perfectly faired outer profile, extending aft to the 10% chord point on the aerofoils. The L-1049 suffered no adverse effect on its performance from the boots and, when necessary, pilots could free the aeroplane from considerable accumulations of ice by turning on the de-icing system.

Super Constellations incorporated a comprehensive electrical system. A number of machines had as many as six, 350A, 30V dc generators fitted. A new type of generator control system was installed which, although developed by Lockheed, was produced by the General Electric Co. and the Hartman Electric Co. This system protected against over-voltage, under-voltage or feeder faults. An advanced, electrical, feeder-fault system was also developed and introduced into the Super Constellation, so that hazards from sparks and electrical faults were virtually eliminated.

Airline customers purchasing a Super Constellation had the choice of two types of the three-bladed variety, one from Hamilton Standard, the other from Curtiss. Hamilton Standard offered the 43E60-9 hub and 6903A-0 blades, which included fluid anti-icing, hydromatic and hydraulic feathering and reverse pitch among its attributes. Curtiss presented their electric type of propeller unit, featuring a C634S-C502 hub and three 858-C-24-0 blades, with reversible pitch and fluid anti-icing. Curtiss also offered the alternative version with a C634S-C504 hub, which differed in having electrically controlled anti-icing. This latter type was chosen by only one airline, Trans Canada. The Curtiss version with fluid anti-icing was specified for KLM, QANTAS, Air India, Seaboard and Western, and Pakistan International. Those airlines choosing Hamilton Standard propellers included, EAL, Iberia Lineas Aereas Espanolas, AVIANCA (Aervias Nacionales de Colombia), LAV (Linea Aeropostal Venezolana), Air France, VARIG SA (Empresa de Viacap Area RioGrandense), Braathens SAFE and Northwest Airlines. Both Hamilton Standard and Curtiss propellers had a diameter of 15ft 2in.

First to purchase the L-1049 Super Constellation was EAL, as they had done with the earlier L-649 model. The first production model (cn.4001), N6201C, entered service on EAL's New York to Miami route on 17 December 1951. This machine, which had made its first flight on 14 July 1951, was the first of fourteen model L-1049s ordered by EAL. A total of twenty-four basic versions of the L-1049 were ordered, with the other ten going to TWA, these having additional centre fuel-tanks, whereas the EAL Super Constellations, flying shorter routes, did not need extra fuel. TWA introduced the L-1049 on their New York to Los Angeles route in September 1952.

A Super Constellation flight deck featuring greater headroom than earlier models, improved control positions, red panel lighting to enhance nocturnal instrument reading and a laminated, electrically heated windscreen to provide improved visibility in adverse weather conditions. In the lower centre of the photograph can be seen the auto-pilot servo for elevator, rudder and aileron control, its three levers being marked E, R, A, respectively.

Despite its four 2,700hp Cyclone engines, the basic L-1049, with its gross take-off weight of 120,000lb, was considered under-powered if any further development of the type was to be undertaken. Strangely, this development began, not with a civil requirement, but through a request from the US Navy. The Korean War was then being fought and the Navy was in need of a long-range military transport possessing increased weight, but having shorter take-off and landing capabilities and, most importantly, a greatly increased power for take-off.

The US Navy, and some other air-arms, had employed the Lockheed P-2 Neptune, maritime patrol-bomber and the ASW aeroplane since 1946. As the P2V-5 (later P-2E), P2V-6 (P-2F) and P2V-7 (P-2H), the very successful Neptune was powered by two, 3,250hp, Wright R-3350-30Ws, and later by a pair of 3,500hp, R-3350-32W, Turbo-Compound, radial engines. Installed in the Neptune, these powerful engines proved a real asset, providing fuel economy, increased speed, improved climb and take-off performance and a longer range. So, when the US Navy approached Lockheed proposing a heavier, more powerful, version of the L-1049 Super Constellation, Wright's R-3350-30W, or 32W, turbo-compound was already available for adaptation. This power-plant had accumulated 12,000 hours of experimental testing and had also proved itself during 160,000 flying hours on tough, rigourous, long, oceanic patrols.

The new engine was, essentially, the same radial as that which powered the earlier Constellations. It was similar to the Lockheed Neptune's engines but, in the form intended for the Super Constellation, it was almost the ultimate in large, piston-type aero-engines. Known as the Wright 972TC 18DA-1, this Turbo-Compound Cyclone was rated at 3,250hp. It was based on a normal Cyclone 18 radial, but with extra power provided by three turbines which operated through the exhausts from six of the eighteen cylinders. These exhaust gases would be wasted on a normal engine but, in

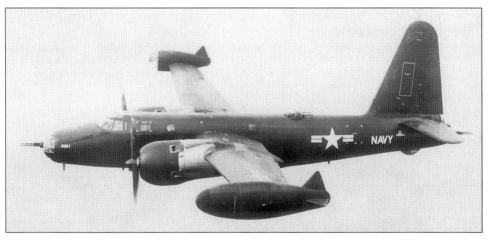

Lockheed's P2V Neptune naval patrol bomber had already proved the reliability of the Wright Turbo-Compound radial, an engine to be fitted to a more powerful version of the L-1049 Super Constellation for military use at the request of the US Navy. This P2V-6 Neptune has been developed from the P2V-5 for mine laying and has no ventral dome.

this new Turbo-Compound, they flowed into the ram, air-cooled turbines before being transferred to the propeller-shaft via the turbine wheel-shaft and the crankshaft. There was no individual control of the turbines but, under any operating conditions, some power was provided. A fluid coupling gave necessary regulation to the motion, enabling the turbine to take advantage of the exhaust energy without any appreciable increase in back pressure. The turbine wheels rotated with a 6.52:1 ratio in relation to the crankshaft speed, whilst the overall dimensions of the engine, compared to an ordinary Cyclone 18, were not great, 11in longer and only $2\frac{1}{2}$in greater in diameter.

A number of features were incorporated into the new Turbo-Compound engines which gave improved longevity of engine-life, thus providing potential users an advantage with regard to extra profitability, due to less hours in the workshop and more hours in the air. These features included: a forged-steel crankcase, which eliminated hundreds of studs and their consequent maintenance; a short, stiff crankshaft, less liable to bend or be subjected to overstressing; stronger and more durable master rods and beatings. Furthermore, a balanced engine air-distribution system, fuel injection, and other refinements, gave valves, pistons and plugs a prolonged life. Up to 85% of the total power was produced by the Turbo-Compound's eighteen cylinders, which operated at 43% of power at cruising speed and gave a 15-20% power increase in the take-off and climb. It was envisaged that previous fuel consumption rates could be maintained, while power was increased by about 20%, or, as an alternative, previous power settings could be retained, thereby giving a saving in fuel consumption of some 20%. The Turbo-Compound was quieter than a conventional engine, the turbining of exhaust gases acted as a miniature muffler. This reduction in engine noise added to passenger comfort.

In this official Lockheed cut-away of an L-1049 Super Constellation the seating arrangements, bulkhead positions, passenger access and baggage loading facilities are clearly shown.

6 Improving The Super Constellation

As such an advanced piston engine was available, Lockheed proceeded to develop an improved L-1049 for the US Navy. Designed as a cargo/troop transport this updated layout featured an integrally stiffened wing, which allowed an eventual increase in maximum take-off weight to 133,000lb. Originally known as the L-1049B, this Super Constellation was given the Navy designation R7V-1 (later C-121 J). It carried a crew of four, along with as many as 106 other personnel. Alternatively it could carry fourteen tons of freight or, as an air ambulance, it could carry forty-seven stretcher-cases and their attendants.

Interest was shown in the Navy's L-1049B/R7V-1 by Seaboard and Western Airlines (later Seaboard World Airlines). They believed the aircraft could help to reduce direct costs in the movement of air freight, as its interior was designed to utilize every inch of available space. It was estimated that a greater tonnage could be moved, with greater ease, than by any contemporary commercial-transport aircraft. They thought the cost of flying freight would work out at around five cents per ton, per mile. Such confidence resulted from the weight-saving and money-saving features incorporated into the all-cargo Super Constellation. These included: an extruded magnesium floor capable of carrying loads of 1,000lb per lineal ft, or 300lb per sq.ft, providing greater latitude in load placement and arrangement; an electric cargo-conveyor and large fore and aft doors, facilitating the simultaneous loading and unloading of cargo. The conveyor device was recessed into the floor of the aircraft to provide maximum, unobstructed, overhead clearance. It was capable of moving an item of freight weighing 12,000lb at a maximum speed of 15ft per minute. To facilitate actual cargo handling, small portable snatch-blocks or pulleys were attached to the standard seat fittings, thus allowing sideways movement of the cargo. This arrangement was quite simple and the effort of loading was limited to sliding the items of freight into an appointed position as they came aboard. By this means, one man was able to load an L-1049B and move the heaviest piece of cargo.

744sq.ft of floor area was available in the main freight compartment, with a further 288sq.ft in the lower freight hold. Thus, a cargo version of the Super Constellation possessed 1,032sq.ft of floor space, an area 29% greater than any contemporary commercial type of aircraft. The floor area was so rigid that the overall area of the load, not the actual contact area, was the determining factor in floor strength. Tie-down fittings were located in a grid pattern across the floor areas so that working loads of 2,400lb each were provided for, in any direction, with no restriction on the angle of pull. A large centre of gravity travel was provided, allowing the widest possible latitude in stowing and unloading freight taken on at intermediate points *en route*. This added further economies in air cargo operations. The large double-door arrangement also minimized loading and unloading times. The huge rear-door (9ft 4½in x 6ft 2⅔in) allowed an item of freight 73ft long, 4ft 1in high and 10in wide to be loaded. The forward door measured 5ft 1½in x 6ft 4¾in.

Powered by four 3,250hp Wright R-3350-34-DA1 Turbo-Compound Cyclone radial piston engines, this L-1049B is a USAF VC-121E, serial 53-7885. It was delivered on 31 August 1954, named Columbine III, *and used as the personal aircraft of President Eisenhower. It was transferred from the US Navy, having been an R7V-1, BuAe No 131650.*

After studying these features of the Cargo Super Constellation, Raymond A.Norden, president of Seaboard and Western Airlines, was full of praise for the type with its 340mph cruising speed. He commented, 'The new airplane will lift more tonnage faster and over greater distances than any other commercial aircraft now flying or in production'. Consequently Seaboard and Western placed an order for four Lockheed L-1049Bs, but this contract was subsequently cancelled in favour of four L-1049Ds, a modified Super Constellation Cargo, very similar to the planned L-1049B civil type, but with heavy-duty flooring installed. This variant had an increased gross take-off weight of 133,000lb in comparison to the L-1049B'S 130,000lb. Total cargo volume was 5,568cu.ft and it could carry a freight load exceeding 36,000lb. The first L-1049D Super Constellation freighter, N6501C, made its initial flight in September 1954, before delivery to Seaboard and Western Airlines (SWA).

Lockheed now had an aircraft 84% heavier than the L-049 when it was first conceived, 54% heavier in gross take-off weight than the first production Constellation, while the TC engines made it 48% more powerful. Furthermore, despite the L-1049D's maximum 133,000lb take-off weight, its airframe was stressed to allow for an all-up weight of 150,000lb.

The L-1049D appeared after the L-1049C, having superseded the L-1049B freighter for Seaboard and Western, but the passenger-carrying L-1049C version of the Super Constellation had structural alterations incorporated to facilitate installation of the Wright 972TC 18DA-1 Turbo-Compound engines. Lockheed strengthened the wing structure, as on the freighter variant, while the interior of the fuselage was updated with an extra 56lb of luxury fittings and added versatility

Seen here on a Lockheed test flight, with the c/n 4501 on its nose, is a Model L-1049C destined for service with the Dutch KLM airline system, hence the registration PH-TFP on the outer fins. It was delivered to KLM on 20 December 1953, the registration being changed later to PH-LKP.

installed. However, the overall empty weight of the aeroplane increased by only 1,584lb. In fact the interior fuselage modifications were such that, despite the new Turbo-Compound engines weighing 2,500lb more than the earlier Cyclone 18s, the L-1049C's fuselage was 1,209lb lighter in weight than the original L-1049 design.

The first of forty-eight L-1049C Super Constellations made its initial flight on 17 February 1953, flown by Lockheed test pilots J. Fales and C.P. Nicholson. This variant carried a crew of six (including cabin staff) and up to ninety-nine passengers. With the Dutch registration PH-TFP (later changed to PH-LKP), this first L-1049C (cn.4501) was one of nine ordered by KLM, which introduced the type on its Amsterdam to New York service in the following August. Other major airlines also placed orders for L-1049Cs, including Air France, EAL, Trans-Canada and TWA.

The L-1049C contained the same fuel capacity as the earlier, basic L-1049 version, which amounted to 5,455 gallons (imperial), but the maximum take-off weight had increased to 110,000lb, as opposed to the earlier variant's 98,500lb. When flying at an altitude of 23,000ft the L-1049C cruised at around 330mph. The range, with maximum fuel and no reserves, was 4,820 miles.

At a time when major fare reductions were running parallel to declining passenger comfort on world air routes, and many air travellers considered they were being conveyed in winged tunnels, Lockheed introduced greater luxury for L-1049C passengers on long-distance flights. The fuselage was compartmentalized and a rest area for crew was located aft of the flight deck, divided from the first, forward

Nice air-to-air shot of Air India International's Lockheed L-1049C, VT-DGL and named Rani of Jhansi.

passenger-cabin by a bulkhead which contained a door for privacy. Beneath the front cabin was a forward, under-floor, freight hold, with a capacity of 728cu.ft. Located at the rear of this front cabin, which seated twelve passengers (two rows of six abreast, each side of the aisle), were port and starboard toilets and wardrobe compartments, followed by the main passenger cabin. Aft of this was a lounge with seats arranged at various angles and beyond this a partition through which one entered a small section with a galley, to starboard. Opposite, there was an entrance door, lobby, ladder-stowage area and a wardrobe. Access to the rear passenger cabin, which contained two-abreast seating, was via another partition and beyond this was a small area for the cabin attendant, with a folding seat and port and starboard wardrobes. Behind this, were two washrooms, partitioned off from the two, rear toilet-compartments situated at the extreme aft end of the cabin area. In those Super Constellations owned by KLM the lounge, with its armchair-style seating, was extremely comfortable and on the cabin walling, large maps showed how the Super Constellation had shrunk the world with its 330mph cruising speed.

Its long-distance capability and luxuriously styled interior made the L-1049C Super Constellation an obvious choice for non-stop transcontinental services. On 19 October 1953, TWA used the type to inaugurate its non-stop Los Angeles to New York route. This competed directly with American Airlines, which was then employing the Douglas DC-7 series, another transcontinental design powered by Turbo-Compound engines, on its long-haul services.

Following the L-1049D cargo version, Lockheed produced the L-1049E, similar to the L-1049C, but which featured modifications increasing the gross take-off weight to 135,400lb, with a landing weight of 113,000lb. A total of twenty-six L-1049Es were ordered but a number were converted, while still on the assembly-line, to a further updated variant, the L-1049G. This was basically an L-1049E powered by Wright 972TC 18DA-3 engines, rated at 3,400hp, a power-plant that became available after Curtiss-Wright had modified the original DA-1 design to include improved supercharging. Consequently, with four DA-3s installed, the L-1049G possessed a maximum combined take-off power of 13,600 bhp, the gross weight of the aircraft having risen to 137,500lb. Landing weight remained the same as the L-1049E and the zero-fuel weight, although initially 104,200lb, was now 108,000lb.

Optional wing-tip fuel tanks could be fitted on the L-1049G Super Constellation, each tank with a capacity of 500 gallons (Imperial). They were the brainchild of designer and chief engineer Clarence L. 'Kelly' Johnson, whose original intention was for them to provide maximum range for a planned turboprop version of the Super Constellation, which never materialized. However, prior to their adoption for the L-1049G, the wing-tip tanks were fitted to the US Navy WV-2, early-warning radar versions of the Super Constellation.

When the L-1049G, or 'Super-G', as it was often known, was fitted with these wing-tip tanks and optional, centre-section, bag-type tanks, its total fuel capacity was

A smiling QANTAS (Australia) Airways captain poses with an L-1049C Super Constellation as he takes delivery on behalf of QANTAS at Lockheed's Burbank plant. The 9ft 6in high nose-wheel gear is apparent in this picture.

Leased to Aerlinte Eireann (later Air Lingus) by the American Seaboard and Western Airline, this L-1049C Super Constellation (N 1005C) was flown between 1958 and 1960 on the Dublin to New York service. It stands here at Dublin Airport. Note the shamrock motif to the rear of the front entrance door.

6,453 gallons (Imperial). Theoretically, the aircraft was capable of a maximum range, in ideal conditions, at 10,000ft, of 4,280 miles. However, more realistically, the range was 4,020 miles, given a headwind of 45mph, reserves for a 230-mile diversion and a possible one-hour stand-off at the destination point.

When the original model L-1049 Super Constellation first arrived on the scene its price was $1.25 million but, by the time the 'Super-G' was produced, the price had risen to more than double that amount. Nevertheless, the Lockheed L-1049G Super Constellation proved to be the best-seller in the Super Constellation range. A total of 104 of this version were produced for the civil market. Northwest Airlines (later Northwest Orient), was the first to fly the 'Super-G', the first delivery being made on 22 January 1955, when N5172V (cn.4572) was handed over. The type entered Northwest's service on 15 February, flying the company's Seattle-Anchorage-Alaska-Tokyo-Okinawa-Manila route. TWA had their L-1049Gs fitted with weather radar facilities and introduced the type on its Washington to London service, on 1 November 1955. Other airlines using the 'Super-G' also had weather radar installed. Although an additional 3ft was required in the nose length to accommodate the radar equipment, it greatly improved safety and comfort for passengers. This radar warned the crew of adverse weather conditions ahead, which could be avoided by course deviation, a factor allowed for by the fitting of long-range, wing-tip tanks, giving an extra 700 mile range. The L-1049G carried up to sixty-three first-class passengers, forty-seven sleeping berths, or ninety-four tourist-class seats and a crew of five to eleven, including cabin staff, depending on whether the route flown was inter-hemisphere.

In the Super 'E' and 'G' Constellations, pilots now had fingertip control over half a ton of advanced electronic equipment, installed to aid the crew, and were provided with the best in contemporary communication and navigational techniques. For example, a transoceanic Super Constellation would be fitted out as follows (subject to an individual airline's requirements): two High Frequency radio transmitter-receivers, serving 100 channels or more; one VHF set for twenty channels; two automatic direction finders; two visual omni-range (VOR) systems, for checking directions from radio ground stations; two glide-path receivers, for instrument landings; one marker beacon, for checking progress along allotted airways; altimeters; interphones and cabin address systems. The large earphones, once clamped to the ears of airline pilots, were phased out on the Super Constellation, being replaced by overhead loudspeakers. The number of these varied in accordance with the requirements of the airline concerned. Some aircraft had speakers located at four, separate flight-stations, and up to twelve installed in the passenger compartments.

Any required maintenance was made easier for the flight deck crew by improved accessibility and quickly removable, electric junction-boxes. Externally, the Super Constellation was subjected to less drag from protuberances by the fitting of low profile antenna. Military-style weather radar was installed on the later Super Constellations, as it became available. This

Another excellent photograph showing the aesthetically pleasing lines of Air India International's L-1049C Super Constellation, VT-DGL, Rani of Jhansi in the early 1960s.

Similar to the L-1049C, the E model had a greater maximum take-off weight. This L-1049E is CF-TGH, fleet number 408, of Trans-Canada Air Lines. Power was provided by four Wright R-3350 Turbo-Compounds.

Also with Trans-Canada Air Lines was this L-1049G Super Constellation, CF-TEU, fleet number 409, seen here running up its R-3350-DA-1 Turbo-Compounds in readiness for take-off.

In full cry above the clouds is L-1049G super Constellation, VH-EAO, named Southern Aurora, *of Australia's QANTAS airways. Powered by four 3,250hp Wright 972-TC-18DA3 Turbo-Compound engines.*

addition to the aircraft's safety equipment included a scanner capable of detecting storms from 50 to 100 miles ahead. It could also provide the crew with information on surface hazards.

Fuel tank arrangements on the Super Constellation were similar to those installed on the earlier L-749A variant, although modifications were made. These included an extra 730 gallon (US) tank, fitted in the unpressurized centre-section of the wing. Located along the top wing surface were seven filler-well openings, one to each tank, which allowed fuel to be added at the rate of 150 gallons (US) per minute each. With the exception of the new centre-section tank, all tanks could be jettisoned, the outer wing tanks being emptied independently by means of hydraulic jettison valves. The four inner wing tanks could be jettisoned two at a time. Fuel from the centre-section tank was transferred to the wing tanks before jettisoning. The fuel tanks were vented by a NACA, non-icing, flush ram-vent. The fuel levels in all seven tanks were indicated on the aeroplane's instrument panel by Simmons Pacitron gauges, or through Liquidometer fuel indicators. On the ground, the amount of fuel in each tank was measured with a dipstick, inserted through the filler-well, while fuel levels in the outer wing tanks and the outer sections of the inner wing tanks could be measured with an auxiliary dipstick.

Lockheed's method of incorporating fuel tanks within the integrally stiffened wing sections of their Super Constellation had a distinct advantage. Firstly, there were fewer holes to seal, which lessened the chance of leaks developing. Secondly, increased strength was obtained with the structure and outer skin of one unit. Thirdly, lighter fuel tanks resulted, despite the increased strength throughout the section. Another asset was the structural integrity used in designing the Super Constellation, which it was envisaged would allow the employment of turboprop engines when they became available.

The German airline Lufthansa also favoured the Super Constellation, here their L-1049G, D-ALAP, shows its paces in a climb. Note the long-range tanks fitted at the wingtips.

The marriage of turboprop engines to a Super Constellation airframe was taken seriously at Lockheed, especially as Pratt & Whitney were making considerable progress in developing their T34 axial-flow type turboprop engine. Plans were already afoot at Lockheed regarding modifications to the aeroplane, so that it could be fitted with T34 engines. These modifications included a reduced wingspan, due to shortening of the wing-tips, strengthening of the landing gear and alterations to the engine control, propeller control, starting systems and oil and fuel supply systems. The flight engineer's panels covering instruments and controls would be improved, while the cabin supercharger arrangement and its controls would be removed. If fitted with turboprop engines, the revised Super Constellation would have a maximum take-off weight of 150,000lb and a landing weight of 110,000lb. Structural zero-fuel weight (gross weight minus fuel) was calculated to be 106,000lb, 6,000lb heavier than the L-1049E. Super-G-type, wing-tip tanks would be fitted to the modified transport when required, giving the proposed L-1249 turboprop variant a total fuel capacity of 7,750 gallons (US). Without the wing-tip tanks total capacity would amount to 6,550 gallons (US). Fuel for the turboprop was of a low-grade quality, similar to kerosene. It was envisaged that, with turboprop power, the L-1249's work capacity would increase from 3,720 ton-mph to 4,760 ton-mph. It was estimated that the average block speed would rise from 315mph to 385mph and the top speed was expected to reach at least 425mph. It was also envisaged, according to Lockheed's calculations, that turboprop power could increase the competitive life of the aircraft by at least four years. The whole idea was based on a minimum cost formula, whereby the turboprop transport aeroplane would be expected to earn substantial profits before, during and after the introduction of long-range, pure-jet transports.

Standing at London Heathrow in the 1960s is a Trans-Canada Air Lines L-1049G Super Constellation, CF-TGB. Note the fleet number, 402, on the fin.

A good close-up of an L-1049G belonging to Lufthansa. The registration is hidden, but a number of details applying to the underneath of the aircraft can be discerned on closer inspection.

Lockheed had already built four turboprop machines for the US military, the R7V-2 (US Navy) and the YC-121F (US Air Force), the latter being two Navy machines which had been transferred. The company planned to stress all L-1049 models for turboprop power from 1954 onwards. Their plans focused on two variants of the L-1249, an 'A' model for cargo and a 'B' model for passenger duties. Both designs would be similar in layout to the L-1049D and L-1049E respectively, except for the new turboprop engines and modified landing gear. Delays occurred at Pratt & Whitney during development of the PT2F-1 (the civil version of the T34 military turboprop engine), but at Lockheed plans and estimates went ahead and were finalized for the L-1249 models. Based on figures obtained for the Navy's R7V-2 version, the results looked quite promising. It was thought that the L-1249A would be able to fly across the US in less than six hours, carrying a sixteen-ton payload, at a cruising speed of 440mph. In theory, it would be capable of flying from Hawaii to California in a similar time, and would be able to make the transatlantic flight from New York to London, via Gander, in an estimated eight hours and forty-five minutes. With a gross take-off weight of 150,000lb the L-1249A would have a service ceiling of 35,800ft. The 8,750 gallon fuel load would be contained in the wing tanks, wing-tip tanks, underwing tanks and tip tanks, the latter two holding 600 gallons apiece. The absolute range was estimated as 4,150 miles and the expected cruising speed was 368mph at 25,000ft. In the case of the proposed L-1249B model, a sea level take-off, at maximum weight, should clear a 50ft high obstacle in a take-off run of 2,900ft. On landing, at a weight of 110,000lb, the L-1249B should be capable of stopping in a distance of 3,500ft after clearing a similar object and carrying out its landing ran. Weighing 110,000lb, the L-1249B was estimated to possess an average block speed of 385mph on a 2,500 mile flight. The top speed in this form was estimated to be 411mph.

Despite its potential, the turboprop version of the Super Constellation did not attract civil buyers and no orders were placed. Even so Lockheed still proceeded with two further projects, in which both the Pratt & Whitney PT2F -1, and the British Rolls-Royce RB100, which would later become the Tyne, were considered.

The first of the two new designs was known as the L-1449. It incorporated a new wing layout, involving laminar-flow, and an increase in wingspan to 150ft. Fuel tanks were still integral with the wing structure, but capacity had now increased to 9,600 gallons (US). There was also a $4\frac{1}{2}$ ft increase in fuselage length, although the maximum weight remained at 150,000lb and the payload worked out at 16,460lb. The maximum range would be well in excess of 5,000 miles and the L-1449's estimated cruising speed was 430mph.

A more advanced project based on the L-1449 was planned at Lockheed, still retaining turboprop engines, but featuring an 11ft 'stretch' to the fuselage. This version was designated the model L-1549, its gross take-off weight was calculated to be 187,000lb, with a payload of some 18,000lb. Its estimated cruising speed was 410mph, at 30,000ft, and the range was expected to be over 4,000 miles. However, there were further delays in the PT2F-1 turboprop programme, resulting in much uncertainty about the engine's availability. Consequently, Lockheed dropped their turboprop ideas for the Super Constellation. The L-1249 programme was cancelled and the L-1449 and L-1549 projects were abandoned. However, the concept as a whole was not a complete loss; from these projects Lockheed employed a number of ideas, especially the revised wing, in a forthcoming venture known as the Starliner.

Meanwhile Burbank's team had taken a hard look at the possibility of a multi-

An L-1049G Super Connie, VH-EAP Southern Zephyr of Australia's airline QANTAS, about to touch down. The optional wingtip tanks increased the aircraft's total fuel capacity to 6,453 imperial gallons, the gross weight with maximum fuel amounting to 137,500lb.

purpose variant of the Super Constellation. As an already well-proven airline type, it was thought the conveyance of passengers or cargo by means of a rapid conversion technique would appeal to operators as an economical proposition. Lockheed went ahead with the new proposal and the resulting model L-1409H prototype (cn.4801) made its first flight on 20 September 1956. Powered by four 3,400hp Curtiss-Wright R-3350-972-TC-18EA-6 Turbo-Compound engines, the L-1049H had a gross take-off weight of 140,000lb. The prototype was later sold to QANTAS and registered VH-EAM. It was followed by a further fifty-two of the same model, ordered by various airlines.

The L-1049H featured a re-stressed and strengthened fuselage designed for a cargo capacity of twenty tons, with a maximum 38,000lb payload being possible on North Atlantic, non-stop, city-to-city flights. This model was an updated, convertible version of the L-1049G, incorporating the special freighting equipment featured in the earlier L-1049D. Conversion to passenger carrying form was rapidly implemented by adding toilets, interior lining panels, racks for cabin luggage, seats for up to 109 tourist-class passengers, a buffet/bar and other passenger requisites. The 'D' type heavy-duty cargo floor was fitted and the 'D' type fore and aft cargo doors were retained. The main freight compartment measured 1,883ft in length and could contain 593cu.ft of bulk loads or individual items of cargo. A second cargo hold was located beneath the main freight area.

The famous Flying Tiger Airlines, an all-cargo concern, employed a substantial number of L-1049H freighters. The last Super Constellation built was delivered to Flying Tiger Airlines during November 1958. This machine (cn.4835) was registered N6925C and carried the airline's fleet number 815. By December 1959 Flying Tiger had acquired a fleet of fourteen L-1049Hs. By 1962 this number was increased to twenty-one machines. This company certainly received good value for money from its L-1049Hs, for they were often working twelve hour per day schedules, with an 84% load factor.

TWA was a champion of both the Constellation and Super Constellation, so it was no surprise when this airline brought a number of L-1049Hs into service. Indeed, on 13 December 1957, TWA carried a record weight of mail on an overseas flight, having fitted out an L-1049H Super Constellation as a special mail-plane. Its purpose was to convey a maximum load of Christmas mail to US military personnel stationed in Germany. No less than 61,000lb of parcels, letters and cards were delivered by that pre-Christmas flight across the Atlantic, of which 23,000lb went to US forces in and around Frankfurt alone.

Until the L-1649A Starliner made its appearance, the Lockheed L-1049H Super Constellation was regarded as the ultimate in long-range transport aeroplanes, in comparison to contemporary types. However, with the advent of jet-propelled airliners, it was acknowledged that a number of the later contracts signed for the L-1049H stipulated it would be employed for passenger-carrying duties as an interim measure only. Obviously, the main factor favouring the L-1049H for airline service, was its value for resale as a cargo type.

This L-1049G Super Constellation is seen when operating in the USA with Seaboard and Western minus wingtip tanks. It was registered N6501C.

Unusual shot from another QANTAS Super Connie of L-1049G, VH-EAD, Southern Dawn. *Notice the QANTAS name painted on the tip tanks.*

The prototype L-1649 Starliner N 1649 (c/n 1001) which first flew on October 11 1956. Developed from the L-1049G Super Constellation, it was powered by uprated 3,400hp Wright Cyclone R-3350-EA2 Turbo-Compounds and introduced a new laminar flow wing.

This L-1049G Super Constellation found itself in service with Air Ceylon as 4R-ACH during the 1960s. Note the wingtip tanks which increased the range (max fuel, full reserves) to over 5,000 miles, a configuration that produced a maximum gross take-off weight of 141,700lb.

The dual-purpose passenger/freighter version of the Super Constellation was the L-1049H, one of which is seen here. Registered N45515, this particular aircraft is in the colours of the famous Flying Tiger Line, a company devoted mainly to cargo operations, and is being towed behind an airport tractor.

This L-1049H, N-1880, is at Miami International Airport in March 1978. It had flown with Lufthansa, Slick Airways, South Pacific Airlines, Alaska Airlines Inc, Conner F.A., Montreal Air Services Ltd and Nordair (Canada). This machine was also leased twice, first to Airlift International and later to World Wide Airways of Canada.

Another well-used L-1049H was N469C seen here at Sebring in March 1978. It appears to be derelict, but it had operated between 1957 and the 1970s (original registration N6636C) with California Eastern Aviation Inc, Slick Airways, Transcontinental SA (Buenos Aires), LEBCA (Linea Expresa Bolivar Compania Anonima, Venezuela), Inter-City Airways (Madrid), was leased to Heiffer Inc (USA) and finally sold to Aerolessors Inc. of Miami.

7 Constellations in Military Service

When the USAAF cancelled its Lockheed C-69 Constellation contracts at the end of the Second World War, twenty-one C-69s had been delivered, or were nearing completion, in military configuration. Among these were eight C-69-1s, ten C-69-5s, and two C-69-1 Os. All were sixty-three seat troop carriers. One machine designated a C-69C (later ZC-69Z) was produced as a forty-three seat VIP transport. Cancelled military variants of the Constellation included: forty-nine C-69C, VIP, high-speed, command transports, with a seating capacity of forty-three; a number of C-69As, with accommodation for up to a hundred troops; several C-69Bs, with seating for ninety-four and three C-69Ds, built to carry fifty-seven personnel. All of these models were designed to carry a crew of six.

In the early post-war years Lockheed was wholly involved with its commercial Constellation programme. No further military interest was shown in the developing airliner until 1948, when the United States Air Force (USAF) showed much interest in the L-749A long-range version, placing an order for ten machines for use as long-range military personnel and freighter transports. Designated C-121As (Lockheed Model 749A-79-38), the new military Constellations were powered by four 2,500hp Wright R-3350-75 radials. Heavy-duty flooring was incorporated for the shipment of cargo and a sizeable freight door in the rear fuselage facilitated the loading and unloading of freight. Alternatively, removable seats could be fitted, as required, to provide a personnel-carrying conversion, or the aeroplane was operable in ambulance configuration with the provision of hospital stretchers.

Three C-121As became VC-121A VIP transports. They were: 48-613, named *Bataan*, for the use of Gen. MacArthur; 48-614, *Columbine I*; 48-610 *Columbine II*, which had a very chequered career. First it was the personal aeroplane of Gen. Dwight Eisenhower, earning the nickname *Gen. Ike's Eagle*, and, as the General was then the commander of NATO, it was stationed in Paris. It flew to most of the major Allied bases and airports in Europe, and quite a number of transatlantic flights were made. The specially chosen crew of eight, led by the pilot, Maj. W.G. Draper, clocked up approximately 50 hours in the air each month.

After its replacement in 1950, by a VC-121 E, *Columbine II* was allocated to Washington DC for VIP duties, returning to Europe, in 1954, as Gen. Gunther's personal machine. It then returned to Washington for another spell of VIP duty, before finally being declared redundant by the USAF. TWA soon purchased 48-610 for their Constellation fleet but later sold it to Ethiopian Airlines, in 1957, as ET-T-35, when it became the personal aeroplane of Ethiopia's Emperor, Haile Selassie. On 10 June that year, while flying near Khartoum, this Constellation met her end when one of the engines caught fire causing the machine to make a forced landing. Fortunately, all those on board escaped, but the Constellation (cn.2602) was burnt out.

A one-off VC-121B (cn.2600) was built as a staff transport, fitted out with a VIP interior and equipped for possible use by the US President. It carried USAF-style

The seventh production Lockheed C-69 Constellation for USAAF service in overall metal finish during World War Two. Just twenty C-69s were sent to USAAF units for war service, this one with serial number 43-10317.

national markings, the serial 48-608 and was named *Dewdrop*. Another six VC-121Bs entered service, but these were all conversions, three C-121As (48-611, -612 and -617) and the three VC-121As mentioned earlier. The remaining C-121As in USAF service flew with the MATS and, for a time, were temporarily reclassified as PC-121As. During the Berlin Airlift, of 1948-1949, the C-121As of the MATS played an important role in helping to convey personnel and essential supplies of food, fuel and other commodities to Tempelhof aerodrome, Berlin. Indeed, in the first month of the Soviet blockade, military Constellations clocked-up over 5 million miles, flying a shuttle service of supplies across the North Atlantic, from the US to Germany.

Meanwhile, developments in radar techniques had been making good progress and the US Navy, wanting to try out the latest early-warning radar and intelligence-gathering electronic equipment, decided the long-range Lockheed L-749A Constellation would provide a suitable testing platform. Consequently, the Navy ordered two of these machines from Lockheed. Initially they were designated PO-1W (later WV-1), the first of which, BuAer No.124437 (cn.2612), made its initial flight in June 1949. The two Airborne Early Warning (AEW) pickets proved quite successful and were soon given the nickname of 'Po Ones'. Massive radomes were fitted above and below the fuselage, the upper protuberance having the appearance of a nuclear submarine's conning tower. A number of antennae were also erected along the top of the fuselage. These radomes, together with their complementary equipment, contained height-finding radar in the top dome and plan-surveillance radar in the lower, teardrop-shaped one. They were designed to seek out enemy aircraft and surface ships in time of war. The crew of twenty-two included aircrew, radar operators and engineers. With their extensive range, both in duration and amount of electronic gear, the PO-1W (WV-1) concept became an accepted and essential part of naval strategy. As for the two original PO-1Ws, apart from interior alterations, the only external difference, to compensate for the additional area taken up by the radome, was an increase in dimensions for the fins.

After the war USAF adoption of the L-749A-79-38 Constellation for military service resulted in the C-121A of which nine were delivered. This particular machine, 48-612, is in USAF/Military Air Transport Service (MATS).

Actually, US Navy faith in the Constellation had already been proved, for initially a naval transport version of the L-049 was ordered as the R70 (Lockheed Model 049-46). No BuAer numbers were allotted, but the type did serve with Navy Squadron VPB-101. Then, with the emergence of the L-1049 Super Constellation, the Navy had invested in the R7V-1, a cargo/troop carrying variant, incorporating a revised wing structure, heavy duty flooring, fore and aft cargo doors and the power of four 3,250hp Wright R-3350-91 Turbo Compound engines. Then, with the favourable reports on the AEW PO-1Ws to satisfy their demands, the Navy placed a production contract for a number of flying radar stations, based on the R7V-1 design. One of these, designated the R7V l-P, was to be equipped with photographic gear and flown on reconnaissance sorties over the Antarctic area. The R7V-1 was also updated to carry a weather-warning radar, installed forward of the flight deck, necessitating an additional 3ft of nose length.

Flying radar pickets were, in fact, airborne electronic sentries, which could extend the range of surface-type radar by great distances. In the aftermath of the Second World War, twenty-three ex-USAAF Boeing B-17G Fortresses were acquired by the US Navy for conversion to airborne radar pickets. Designated PB-1W, these B-17Gs had extra fuel tanks installed, a large 'guppy' type radome fitted into the bomb bay and, when the APS-20 search radar was installed, defensive armament was removed. Two B-29 Superfortresses were also transferred from the USAAF to the Navy as P2B-1 flying radar pickets, with additional fuel capacity and search radar contained in the bomb bay. The following Lockheed PO-1W trials paved the way for a diverse series of military types based on the Turbo-Compound powered Super Constellation, which after the 1962 US Forces aircraft re-designation system, became the EC-121 with suffixes up to the letter T.

The new AEW Super Constellations entered US Navy service during the mid-1950s as PO-2Ws, later WV-2 (EC-121K in 1962), and were allotted the official

Carrying a 'speedpack' freight container beneath its fuselage, this USAAF C-69-5 (42-94559) was later converted by Lockheed to L-049 standard for civil use and sold during 1946 to BOAC as G-AHEN Baltimore.

name 'Warning Stars'. Four uprated 3,400hp Wright R-3350-34 or 42 Turbo-Compound Cyclone 18s provided the power. Wing-tip tanks, similar to those on the civil 'Super-G', allowed for a maximum possible range, with a duration of up to thirty hours. The crew of twenty-six included a number of radar operators, who sat facing an array of consoles and radarscopes, involving nearly six tons of radar, electronics, data links and special communication systems employed in AEW operations. These ocean-going AEW aircraft included bunks among the furnishings, to enable members of the crew to take a rest from duty, although about half the cabin space contained the radar and much of its complementary equipment. Even so, a galley was incorporated, allowing the off-duty crew to preparing hot meals and drinks. A good supply of spare components was carried by each WV-2/EC- 121K, so that any necessary running repairs could be carried out while the aircraft was still on patrol.

Conversions were undertaken to a number of WV-2s, which were fitted out with sophisticated electronic countermeasures (ECM) equipment, direction finding (DF), jamming devices, and additional aerials and antennae aft. Initially designated WV-2Qs, these machines became EC-121Ms, in accordance with the revised military aircraft classification system of 1962.

One WV-2, BuAer No.126512 (cn.4301), was equipped with a new aerial surveillance radar system known as AN/APS-82, the aircraft being re-designated as a WV-2E (later EC-121L). This equipment was housed in a large nine-ton rotating dish, atop a massive pylon embodied in the aircraft's upper fuselage. In this configuration the WV-2E made its initial flight during 1956, but the EC-121L did not reach production status. However, a rotodome dish-scanner was fitted to a Grumman WF-2 Tracer, a combination that was accepted by the US Navy, albeit for use aboard aircraft carriers.

Put out to grass in Pima County, November 1976, an ex-VIP staff transport, USAF serial 0-80614. It was initially a C-121A (military variant of the L-749A), but later modified to become a VC-121A. It was given the name Columbine I, *later becoming a VC- 121B.*

A number of World War Two Boeing B-17G Flying Fortresses were later transferred to the US Navy and converted into flying radar pickets with the designation PB-lW. This overall dark blue machine was USAAF 44-83874 before acquiring Navy BuAe No 77237. The 'guppy' under-belly radome is prominent in this picture.

Fine air-to-air shot of a US Navy Lockheed WV-2 Warning Star flying radar station, re-designated in 1962 as an EC-121K. Note the locations of the upper and lower radar housings and antenna.

The Navy also received nine, special weather-reconnaissance versions of the Super Constellation, designated the WV-3 (later WC-121N). Eight were produced, BuAer Nos137891-137898 (cns 4378-4385). The remaining machine was a WV-2, BuAer No.141323 (cn.4447), converted to WV-3 configuration. The last two of the eight newly-built machines, BuAer numbers 137895 and 137898, were later transferred to the USAF and became EC-121Rs, 67-1471 and 67-1472, respectively.

The WV-3 weather machines, although employing the same basic airframe as the WV-2, together with the large radome and ventral 'guppy' dome, contained a different internal layout, in which the plotting crew numbered only eight, while the wing-tip fuel tanks were omitted. Earning the nicknames *Storm Seeker* and *Hurricane Hunter*, the nine WV-3s used a type of radar capable of covering over 190,000 square miles of ocean in one sweep. Operating with Navy Squadron VW-4, these weather-seeking Super Constellations flew from the US Naval Air Station at Roosevelt Roads, Puerto Rico, and from Jacksonville, Florida.

Meanwhile, the proposed fitting of four turboprop engines to a Super Constellation certainly interested the US Navy. It was decided at Burbank, in 1952, to produce a Super Constellation powered by four 5,500ehp Pratt & Whitney YT34-P-12A turboprop engines, driving Hamilton Standard Turbo Hydromatic propellers, of 15ft in diameter, featuring three paddle-type blades, each 2ft wide. The Navy ordered four turboprop Super Constellations, aware that the R7V-2, as it would be designated, would emerge as perhaps the world's fastest propeller-driven transport aircraft at that time. The first R7V-2 made its initial flight on 1 September 1954. By the summer of 1955 all four machines were flying. This model featured wing-tip fuel tanks, each containing 600 gallons (US), which complemented the main tanks to provide a maximum fuel capacity of 8,750 gallons (US). Gross take-off weight was 150,000lb and the service ceiling was 35,800ft. During take-off the Pratt & Whitney T34s were on full power, at 11,000rpm, but, because of a very efficient gear-reduction arrangement, the large propellers rotated at only 1,000rpm.

One of the US Navy's Lockheed L-1049Bs (Navy designation WV-2 and later EC-121K), of which 124 were produced as an Airborne Early warning version of the Super Constellation. The dorsal 'fin' radar dome and ventral 'guppy' dome/scanner between them housed several tons of electronic equipment.

The R7V-2 was considered to be quite a viable proposition, with great military and commercial potential, but surprisingly little interest was shown in the type and no production contract was forthcoming. The four R7V-2s built remained in the category of test aircraft and were allotted BuAer numbers 131630, 131631, 131660 and 131661 (cns 4131, 4132, 4161 and 4162, respectively). However, in 1956 the latter two machines were transferred to the USAF as YC-121Fs, with the serials 53-8157 and 53-8158. One of the two remaining Navy R7V-2s later served as a flying test-bed with four, 3,750ehp, Allison 501-D13 turboprop engines and nacelles fitted, as used on Lockheed's Model L-188 Electra airliner.

Another two Navy variants were the NC-121Ks. These were converted EC-121Ks and EC-121Ps. The EC-121Ks were converted for special purpose tests and projects, including 'Birdseye', the ASWEPS programme, and 'Magnet', in which the earth's magnetic field was studied and mapped out. The EC- 121Ps were a batch of EC- 121K conversions, equipped for anti-submarine warfare (ASW), their interiors containing ASW sensors and Navaids, for operations under water. Additionally, a substantial number of US Navy R7V-1 (later C-121 J) transports were transferred to the USAF, which was another major operator of military Super Constellations.

After the success of its C-121As, the USAF ordered the L1049 Super Constellation during 1951, designating it the C-121C, for long-range transport duties. Seventy-five personnel, fourteen tons of freight, or forty-seven stretcher cases could be carried, as dictated by circumstances. Four 3,500hp Wright R-3350-34 Turbo-Compound radials powered the Lockheed C-121C, which had a maximum take-off weight of 135,400lb, an increase of 28,400lb over the earlier C-121A model. Like the Navy, the USAF saw the Super Constellation as ideal for the AEW role, and the Air Force initially ordered ten, designated the RC-121C. These USAF flying radar pickets carried some 15,000lb of radar equipment, including ANAPS-20 search

Equipped with AN/APS-82 aerial surveillance radar contained in a large rotating dish weighing some nine tons, this Lockheed WV-2E (later EC-121 L) BuAe No 126512 first flew in 1956 but did not reach production status.

In overall dark blue this US Navy Lockheed WV-3, BuAe No 137894, coded 'MH', when operating with Navy Squadron VW-4.

radar and APS-42 cloud collision gear. The aircraft was similar in profile to the Navy WV-2, possessing the upper and lower radome layout. The 8ft vertical dome above the fuselage housed the height-finding antenna, while the lower 'guppy' ventral dome contained the bearing scanner. No wing-tip tanks were fitted to RC-121Cs but, with a maximum load, the endurance at a cruising speed of 335mph was twenty-four hours, given reasonable weather conditions. Designated EC-121C in 1962, these RC-121Cs had entered USAF Air Defence Command service during 1953. They were employed mainly on patrol duties along the western seaboard of the US.

May 1954 saw the first of seventy-two RC-121D Warning Stars (later EC-121D) delivered to the USAF. These updated machines featured wing-tip auxiliary fuel tanks, resulting in a longer operating range, and they were fitted out with improved AEW equipment and electronics. RC-121D/EC-121D Warning Stars were employed as long-range patrol aircraft, or as a flying control centre for the guidance of interceptor fighters. They were known as AEW & C (Airborne Early Warning & Control) aircraft. This variant was the basis for several other types of advanced electronics and surveillance aircraft. Its maximum take-off weight was now an impressive 143,000lb.

With the designation EC-121D, applied in 1962, the Warning Stars had a computer and other modified electronic equipment added, so that the type was able to operate with other forces committed to defending North America under the NORAD/SAGE (North American Air Defence/Semi-Automatic Ground Environment) programme. As more sophisticated radar and electronics were developed, no less than forty-two EC-121DS received considerable internal modifications, in which SAGE data links, an advanced airborne computer, revised navaids and other updated electronic equipment were installed. Distinguishable by having a small, streamlined radome located on top of the fuselage, just ahead of the main dome, this version was designated the EC-121H.

The majority of AEW &C aircraft flew with the USAF (ADC) 551st Airborne Early Warning & Control Wing, which operated out of Otis Air Force Base (AFB), Massachusetts. In their more sophisticated configuration, they were used to feed information to NORAD (North American Air Defence) surface bases. Several

The Lockheed Model L-1249 (US Navy R7V-2), powered by four 5,700shp Pratt & Whitney T-34 turboprop engines (YT-34-P-12A). It was one of only four built, its BuAe No being 131660. The Navy retained two machines and the remaining two transferred to the USAF as YC-121Fs.

machines were converted as TC-121C radar crew trainers, but these aircraft later reverted to their original EC-121C configuration. Two EC-121Ds (cns 4334 and 4410), with USAF serials 52-3416 and 55-137, respectively, featured special, classified, electronics equipment and were designated EC-121Js. Another operator of Warning Stars was the 552nd AEW & C Wing of the USAF based at Sacramento, California. This unit took delivery of four EC-121Q aircraft, which were EC-121Ds specially adapted for AWACS (Airborne Warning & Control System) operations.

During the Vietnam War, three types of ground sensors were employed to relay information back to American forces. Two types buried themselves in the ground, leaving just the antenna above the surface, and one was attached to a parachute, intended to hang from trees. The sensors were dropped either from fast, low-flying jets, or from slow, twin-engine aircraft. Their intelligence signals were picked up by specially modified Lockheed EC-121K/EC-121P Super Constellation relay stations, designated EC-121R. Thirty of this variant were supplied for these operations, which were known as Project Igloo White. Their upper and lower radomes were omitted, but wing-tip fuel tanks were fitted. They were in a tactical camouflage finish.

The choice of EC-121Rs for use in Project Igloo White was due to the type's ability to fly low-level missions for up to twenty hours, if necessary, at the same time keeping an accurate course to stay within receiving range of the signals emitting from the ground sensors. The EC-121R crew then relayed any information received from the sensors to an Infiltration Surveillance Centre (ISC) in Thailand. If a delay occurred in relation to ISC processing when a vital target was involved, the EC-121R was able to send the required information direct to attack aircraft, already airborne.

The US Navy and Air Force received more than 220 main variants of the Super Constellation. The interiors of many were completely re-equipped with updated

Powered by four Wright R-3350-34 Turbo-Compounds, this Lockheed Model L-1049B (C-121C) is seen serving with the USAF/MATS, US-Europe, Atlantic Division, which operated mainly between the United States and Europe. Its serial number is 54-151.

Lockheed Model L-1049s and USAF RC-121s under completion at Burbank. Note the Navy P2V Neptunes and a couple of visiting Douglas DC-3s. Compare this view with that of the 1929 site shown earlier.

electronics, while others underwent a re-building programme. A number of the less electronically sophisticated versions of the Super Constellation continued operating with US Air Defence Command into the 1970s, several serving with the 79 Air Reserve Squadron (915th AEW & CG), flying from the Air Force Base at Homestead, Florida, on Atlantic patrol duties. Aircraft used by this unit during the late 1970s included the EC-121T, a modified version of the EC-121D, for use as an 'Elint' electronic intelligence platform, incorporating a computerized AEW & C feedback system. The large dorsal radome and its equipment were omitted, while a cooling air intake was incorporated beneath the forward fuselage. The EC-121T was the heaviest of the Super Constellations, with a gross take-off weight of 152,000lb. At least twenty-four of these aircraft are believed to have been delivered. EC-121Ts were last in the Warning Star series, some of them being deployed from Keflavik, Iceland, until 1978.

A handful of EC-121Ts retained their large radomes, and it was one of these, 54-2307 (cn.4389), which had the distinction of being one of the last Warning Stars in service.

As a purely military transport vehicle, the Super Constellation served with the US Navy, USAF and the Air National Guard (ANG) in its C-121C and C-121G variants. One of the type's primary roles was as an air ambulance and for casualty evacuation. A rather bizarre colour scheme was applied to one Navy EC-121M, BuAer No.135756 (cn.4323), which was attached to the US Navy Pacific Missile Range Squadron. It had a white upper fuselage and radome, orange/red (day-glo) front fuselage, tail unit and rear fuselage, and black rudders and nose cone. The remainder of the aircraft was in US Navy blue finish, with 'Navy' in white lettering on the fuselage sides and beneath the port wing. Another Navy Super Constellation, BuAer 131642(cn.4143), later went to the USAF as C-121G, number 54-4065, and was leased to the National Aeronautics & Space Administration (NASA) for use by the Goddard Space Flight Centre. This was in connection with the evaluation of tracking equipment concerning the Mercury, Gemini and Agena projects and flights. Based in Australia from May to October 1966, this C-121G later returned to the US and was initially registered as NASA20. It later became NASA420 before eventually transferring to the US Army for employment at a Maryland proving ground.

Super Constellations also flew with the Indian Air Force (IAF), in the form of nine, L-1049 'Super-G' types acquired from Air India. Eight were for use in the maritime reconnaissance (MR) role and one was a military transport. The reconnaissance machines flew with No.6 (MR) Squadron of the IAF, but despite their ability to fly long distance patrol duties, they could only provide limited information on the movement of surface ships. These IAF Super-Gs were controlled by the Indian Maritime Air Operations Directorate of 1971, which could also call in attack aircraft for interdiction duties.

The RC-121D Airborne Early Warning (AEW), an updated version of the RC-121 C, with wingtip tanks, additional internal fuel capacity and a crew of 31 personnel. Engines were 3,500hp Wright Cyclone R-3350-75-DA1 Turbo-Compounds. In 1962 this model was re-designated EC- 121D. USAF serial was 53-539.

Landing at Mildenhall, UK, on 28 August 1978, is USAF EC-121T, No.54-2307, of the AFRES/79th AEW and Control Squadron, from Homestead, Florida, USA. This particular aircraft was one of the last operational Warning Stars and also one of the few to retain its dorsal dome.

Again at Mildenhall, two days earlier, is the USAF (AFRES) EC-121T, 54-2307, its dorsal radome and ventral 'guppy' dome positions clearly visible in this picture. Note the 'guppy' dome's close proximity to the ground.

Another Mildenhall visitor was this EC-121T, 52-3414, USAF (AFRES). In this case the dorsal radome has been removovd as it was on a number of the Warning Stars in USAF service.

Pure transport version of the military Super Connie was the C-121 C, like this one of the USAF, Air National Guard, New Jersey, serial 040171.

An EC-121 S, 54-0155, of the USAF at Lackland Air Force Base, waiting restoration for display purposes.

Here the same EC-121S (54-0155) has been completely refurbished, and is in C-121C configuration. This 1983 picture shows the aircraft displayed at Lackland AFB, main gate. Note the main wheel clamps!

8 Starliner Constellation
Par Excellence

The Super Constellation's development programme entered into a battle of the giants. When Lockheed introduced their L-1049C, Douglas Aircraft Corporation came up with the DC-7, built in response to a request from American Airlines, who considered TWA's Super Constellations as a serious threat to their own transcontinental traffic. Douglas then went ahead with the DC-7C 'Seven Seas', with increased wingspan and additional fuel capacity, which made it capable of flying non-stop transatlantic flights in both directions. This aircraft proved a great success for Douglas, and Pan American introduced the type into service on 1 June 1956, the first of several major airlines to employ DC-7Cs.

In turn, TWA requested an updated Super Constellation from Lockheed, to compete with the DC-7C. This resulted in Lockheed's L-1649A Starliner, a larger more sophisticated variant than the Super-G, its immediate predecessor. Indeed, the Starliner was the ultimate in four-engine piston airliner design and performance, as well as being the biggest aircraft of this class produced in the US for regular airline service. Compared to the Super Constellation, the Starliner was virtually a new design, but the very low level of engine noise in the cabins, while reminiscent of the soundproofed Super-G, was mainly due to engine relocation. In contrast, the Super-G incorporated extra insulation and modified propellers, in which the tip speeds were slowed, resulting in a much quieter interior, even in those seats located nearest the inboard engines.

The superiority of the L-1649A over its predecessor was mainly due to a new laminar flow wing, redesigned functional systems and improved engines, in the form of four 3,400hp Wright R-3350-988TC-18EA-2 Turbo Compounds, driving three-blade Hamilton Standard Hydromatic propellers featuring reverse pitch. All of these features were intended to produce a new standard of performance, comfort and dependability. Nevertheless, as Lockheed pointed out, despite the numerous changes, similarity with earlier variants of the Constellation had been retained as far as possible. No major cockpit design or procedural alterations were carried out, maintenance and repairs to the engines differed very little from that employed on the Super Constellation, and the basic concepts of components and systems did not alter radically from previous configurations.

Undoubtedly the most important element in the Starliner's more advanced performance and capabilities, was the newly designed laminar flow wing, with its span of 150ft, 27ft greater than that of the L-1049G. The aspect ratio was 12:1, opposed to the 9.71:1 of earlier Constellations, but the dihedral angle of 7°30' was the same for both the early Super Constellations and the Starliner. The L-1649A wing was located further aft along the fuselage than that of the L-1049G and, with its large machined parts, it became the nearest to contemporary one-piece construction

Success of the Douglas DC-7C airliner prompted TWA to request that Lockheed update the Super Constellation in order that it could seriously compete with the Douglas type. This Douglas DC-7C was G-AOIA Seven Seas, *of BOAC and is seen in the 1950s on a pre-delivery test flight.*

attained in a component of that size. This resulted in many detail parts and hundreds of rivets being eliminated, while at the same time there was a marked improvement in the ratio of strength to weight.

This new laminar flow wing was constructed from two panels, with a joint at the centreline of the aircraft. Because of the beam length, the front and rear beams had to be spliced at a specific wing station, namely WS265.680, and the upper and lower skins at WS468.50. The beam webs were spliced at wing stations WS505.50 and WS595.00, respectively. It was emphasized that none of the splices were designed as service joints but, in the event of damage to the left or right wing panel, it was possible to replace the panel by dismantling the manufacturing joints.

Ample space was provided in the wing for integral fuel tanks, the front beam being situated at 15% and the rear beam at 63.5% of the chord. Thus, with an additional 27ft of wing span and the beam spread, the L-1649A possessed a greater fuel capacity than the L-1049G. In fact, the Starliner contained a maximum fuel load of 9,728 gallons (US), giving a range of 4,940 miles.

The L-1649A Starliner's laminar flow wing structure and detailing is in itself a subject worthy of special attention. It consisted of upper and lower skins incorporating spanwise 'planks'. These were milled from extrusions, or plates, and included integral stiffeners. Both the front and rear beam assemblies comprised a lower beam cap with an upright leg, forming about one-third of the total beam web height, and a machined web-plate, to which the upper and lower beam caps were attached. The result was a very effective fail-safe design. The Starliner's wing box structure incorporated truss-type ribs, composed of extruded truss members and extruded caps, the ribs being attached to the integral stiffeners of the upper and lower wing panels by 'H'-clips, a method which eliminated the use of fasteners through the integral fuel tank walls. The tank-end ribs were formed from integrally stiffened, extruded webs and extruded upper and lower caps. The rib caps were riveted to machined flats, on the inner surface of the skin, and no stringer seals were necessary. To prevent any possible fuel leakage, several improvements were made to the fuel tank access panels and adjacent structure, while the box beam construction used faying-surface sealing extensively within the integral tanks and no structural compromise was required. All integral tanks were sealed by the latest contemporary sealants, and fill and drain operations. A panel in the upper surface of the port wing provided access to the compass wiring plugs.

The main landing gear support ribs, each a single forging, were located in the dry bay, behind the inboard engine nacelles, and away from the fuel tank area. Access to this dry bay was through a panel in the rear beam, directly aft of each

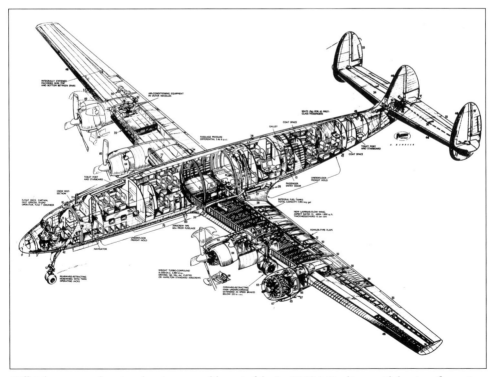

Official cut-away drawing showing general layout of the L-1649A Starliner, with laminar flow wing, seating arrangements and construction details.

Prototype Lockheed L-1649 Starliner powered by four 3,400hp Curtiss-Wright R-3350-EA2 Turbo-Compound engines. First flight was on October 11 1956, and it entered TWA service on 1 June 1957.

dry bay section. Two smaller panels, situated in the rear beam, allowed the dry bays to be inspected from outside. All external access panels for the fuel tanks were similar to those of the Super-G Constellation, but on the Starliner they were incorporated into the top of the wing.

The L-1649A Starliner's wing leading edges were sectionalized, with two extending from the wing roots to the outboard nacelle. These were hinged at the upper beam cap, opening upwards and providing easy access to piping, wiring and other equipment fitted to the front wing beam. Three hinged leading edge sections, with hinges fitted at both the top and bottom, were located between the outboard engine nacelles and the wing-tips. These leading edge sections could be removed by pulling out a series of stainless steel hinge-pins, which were relatively short and dry-film lubricated. Those hinge-pins on the two inboard sections were attached to a small plate, which, in turn, was fixed to the wing with quick-opening fasteners, in order to ensure pin retention. When the hinge-pin was removed a red patch was revealed, which was not covered completely until the pin and plate were correctly re-installed. To allow for the chordwise de-icer boot installations used, each leading edge section was recessed and, as these were easily removed, replacement of de-icer boots could take place on the workshop bench.

Skinning on the wing trailing edges consisted of panels assembled by means of a metal-bonding process, known as Scotchweld, in which the top skin consisted of a smooth outer sheet bonded to a beaded inner sheet. The bottom skin also consisted of two bonded sheets. Attached to the underneath of the trailing edge skin, were a number of closure pans for controlling air flow between the upper surface of the wing flaps and the trailing edge itself. This idea reduced drag and tended to improve lift, by narrowing the gap between the trailing edges and the flaps. When the wing flaps were fully extended for servicing purposes, all equipment fitted to the rear beam face was accessible for maintenance and inspection. Additionally, eleven hinged and Cam-Loc fastened access panels were located along the lower trailing edges of each wing. With the trailing edge ribs being spaced 18-24in. apart, there was enough room available for maintenance purposes. Manufactured as a single unit the wing-tip was 28in. long and was secured to the main wing by means of four tension bolts. A hinged panel in the upper skinning provided access to these bolts, as well as to the navigation light plugs and compass transmitters.

Of semi-monocoque construction, the engine nacelles were integral with the wing structure, but structurally independent of the wing leading edge. They were fitted to the wing front-beam by means of a shear and tension structural joint. Their main internal framework was formed from 17-7PH steel, while the flat-wrapped skinning was fabricated from 302 full hard stainless steel. The spot-welding technique was employed in the construction of each nacelle, while the main landing gear doors on the inboard nacelles were formed from stainless steel skin fitted over an aluminium sub-structure. Engine oil was added from the tops of all the nacelles. The outboard nacelles also featured an alcohol service filler on their tops, with access to the air-conditioning equipment being located below and to the rear.

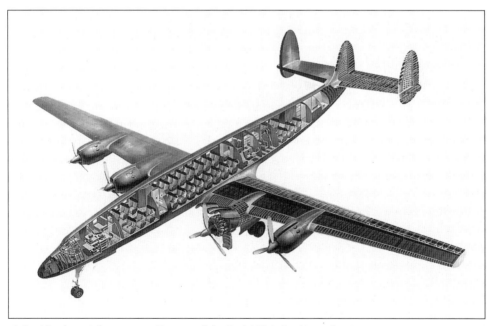

A Lockheed special cut-away diagram of the L-1649A Starliner, showing compartments, passenger and crew seating arrangements and structure details.

Fire protection was obviously high on the list of priorities in the construction of aircraft, especially where passenger-carrying types were involved. In the case of the L-1649A Starliner, Lockheed certainly went to great lengths to prevent any possible fire spreading from one area to another around the nacelles. Compartments and barriers were incorporated, the inboard nacelles having a fireshield of stainless steel installed 15in. forward of the front wing-beam. This covered the front beam installations, but was quite easily removed for maintenance and inspection purposes. As for the outboard nacelles, they had fireshielding composed of several small, stainless steel sections spaced around 1in. from the front wing-beam. As an added precaution, equipment fitted to the front wing beam, in the fire zone, was built from fire-resistant materials. Further safety measures, to counteract any possible fire-threat, included the fitting of closed trailing edge ribs on either side of each nacelle and outboard of the cabin heater, while closure was provided between the wing and fuselage in the aft service-area compartment. Other fire-prevention measures included: closed leading edge ribs, just outboard of the wing and fuselage fillet; closed fillet bulkheads, situated over the box-beam near the front and rear wing beams and closed leading edge ribs on either side, in the stub leading edge portion of each nacelle.

The main attachment points for marrying the wing to the fuselage were located on the bottom ends of the circular, fuselage bulkhead-frames. These were fitted

As mentioned earlier, TWA introduced the L-1649A Starliner into service on 1 June 1957 naming it their Jetstream class. Here the second Starliner built (c/n 1002) is with TWA as N7301C, fleet number 301.

An Air France L-1649A Starliner, F-BHBK, with its Curtiss-Wright R-3350-EA2 Turbo-Compounds in full cry as it carries out a pre-delivery test flight off the Californian coast.

fore and aft onto the front and rear wing beams. Machined pads in each of the bulkhead-frame ends were joined to forgings bolted to the exposed face of the beams. Double attaching bolts were used (two double-bolts for each of the four attachments) to afford the maximum in fail-safe design. This amounted to a bolt within a bolt, meaning that if one bolt failed, the second was capable of carrying the design load. Inspection of these special attaching bolts was accomplished either by removing the wing-to-fuselage filet sections, or by means of cabin floor inspection covers. To enable handling of the complete wing assembly, both during manufacture and in the field, hoist fittings were incorporated into the structure. Also, the whole 150ft-span unit, complete with nacelles, could be moved on a special trailer, fitted with wing support mountings, the motive power being provided by a towing tractor.

Fuel was contained in seven tanks an outer, centre and inner tank in each wing and the seventh tank in the aircraft's centre-section, where it was divided by the port and starboard wing joint. The fuel was distributed across the entire wing span, with the exception of the dry areas aft of each inboard engine. Each wing-tank contained some 1,350 gallons (US), while the centre-section tank held 1,600 gallons (US), of 115/145 grade gasoline. A vented, vapour-tight, neoprene blanket (septum) separated the upper surfaces of the wing from the fuselage, in order to prevent fumes from entering the cabin area should a leak occur in the centre-section fuel tank. Electrically-operated fuel booster pumps were mounted in the lower wing, at the aft end, inboard of each tank. These pumps delivered fuel to

The laminar flow wing is prominent in this view of an L-1649A Starliner (Super Star) of the German airline Lufthansa, its registration D-ALUB.

the engine-driven pumps at pressures of between 19 and 35lb per sq.in. Fuel could be supplied from any tank to any engine, or combination of engines, by means of a cross-feed system. The design also prevented an inter-tank transfer of fuel from occurring and placed all fuel and vent plumbing within the confines of the box area of the wing.

As previously mentioned, the L-1649A Starliner appeared as a virtually new aircraft but retained a number of features of the L-1049G Super Constellation. For example, the 28V dc, single-wire electrical system was very similar, with the airframe structure acting as a common ground, although this was not utilized at the flight station circuits, these having two wires to eliminate any possible compass deviation. However, the L-1649A employed a secondary 115V three-phase, 400-cycle ac system.

There was little difference in the air-conditioning between the Super-G and the Starliner. The air-distribution, pressurization, cooling, heating and ventilation systems were all similar. However, some accessories differed in their location and installation. For instance, on the L-1649A Starliner the main body of the refrigeration system was situated in the outboard, lower nacelles, aft of the wing-front, beam bulkhead. As in the Super-G, the cabin supercharger was located in

On 10 April 1955, F-BHBR, an L-1649A Starliner of Air France, was at Anchorage, Alaska, on the inauguration of Air France's polar route to Japan (Tokyo) – a thirty hour flight.

the outboard nacelles (zone No.3), supported by a welded tube-bracket fixed to the wing-front beam. Due to the Starliner's different wing structure, the two cabin heater units, similar to those on the L- 1049G, were installed further forward and reversed from their position on the Super-G. Another heater unit, which was installed on one side of the L-1049G, was fitted on the opposite side of the L-1649A, and was reversed end for end.

Two 3,000lb per sq.in. main hydraulic systems were used in the Starliner, supplemented by two electrically-driven auxiliary units. This layout, while achieving the quick action of hydraulic equipment, allowed a reduction in the size and weight of major components, a factor noticeably apparent in the case of the landing gear actuating cylinders. Variable-displacement pumps, driven by engines one and three, operated the number one hydraulic system, while system number two was powered from engines two and four.

The new laminar flow wing did not allow the installation of the earlier type of aileron control-boosters in the L-1649A. Lockheed wanted to provide the Starliner with a revised booster unit, featuring improved performance and maintenance characteristics. They produced the L-1649A control booster system, an updated form of the booster system installed in the Lockheed C-130 Hercules transport. It could be fitted as a basic unit at the aileron, elevator or rudder positions. The hydraulic components of this booster were grouped in a manifold that could easily be removed from the booster unit, facilitating a bench-check or possible replacement. Lockheed promised exceptional reliability from all three boosters, as each featured a dual, tandem actuating-cylinder, operated from both hydraulic systems. A single booster unit was employed for both ailerons on the Starliner, located in the rear, unpressurized section of the lower fuselage. This lone booster operated the ailerons via push-pull tubes supported by rollers. The L-1649A's hydraulic system also featured a PB-20A autopilot, which had electro-hydraulic controls linked to the booster's hydraulic manifold.

The Starliner's wing-flaps relied heavily on the aircraft's hydraulic system for their operation, having been redesigned to employ two flap-sections on each wing, with the individual sections actuated by two ball bearing screw jacks and intermediate gearbox units mounted in the wing trailing-edges. Newly designed carriages and tracks were incorporated for the movement of the Lockheed-Fowler flaps, which were operated by two hydraulic motors through a main gearbox. Each of these motors was driven separately by one of the two main hydraulic systems, while a torque-tube arrangement linked the drive motors and intermediate gearbox units. Flap positions were selected from the flight deck via a cable system connected to a follow-up device mounted on the main gearbox.

The L-1649A had a gross take-off weight of 156,000lb. This made it necessary to design a completely new main landing gear. The new units acquired redesigned locking mechanisms. If there was a failure of the hydraulic system the uplocks on all three landing gears could be opened by manual release. It is interesting to observe that the main gear legs were designed for use as a speed-brake, at speeds of up to 269mph. The nose wheel landing gear on the L-1649A remained essentially the same as that on the 'Super G' Constellation, except for two

Lufthansa owned four Lockheed L-1649A Starliners. This one, hurrying along above the clouds, was registered D-ALER.

actuating cylinders provided on the Starliner, each of which was operated separately by one of the two main hydraulic systems.

Because of the L-1649A's increased wingspan, the engine nacelles were moved out a distance of 5ft, which had the consequent effect of reducing interior cabin noise. This factor was further improved with the installation of additional soundproofing material and synchrophasing of the Hamilton Standard propellers. These three-blade metal propellers had a diameter of 16ft 10in, but a tip to fuselage clearance of 5ft. The introduction of a slower rate of revolutions per minute reduced the blade-tip speed, resulting in lowering the audible sound.

The whole empennage on the Starliner was essentially similar to earlier models of the Constellation, with the exception of the tailplane chord, which was slightly increased. However, some structural changes were necessary so that new reinforcing members could be installed to support the rudder and elevator hydraulic booster units introduced on this model. Counterbalances were transferred from the control horns to the tops of the rudders, below the uppermost hinges. Other tailplane updates included strengthening the stabilizer beams and making minor changes to the leading-edge structure and rudder torque-tubes.

Because of its weather-radar, contained within the matt-black, non-metal cone attached to the Starliner's extreme front pressure-bulkhead, the L-1649A was 2ft 7in. longer than the earlier L-1049C Super Constellation. This aircraft required

Unusual night scene at Orly airport, Paris, as L-1649A Starliner, F-BHBL, prepares for a trans-Atlantic flight to New York during the late 1950s.

considerable redesigning, mainly because of the need to accommodate its laminar flow wing and adjust to the type's maximum weight. Much of this work involved that part of the fuselage known as number 4 section. Originally barrel-shaped, it was altered to have a cross-section that was of constant diameter. In addition, section 5A, aft of section 4, had to be re-faired, so that it would match up to the revised shape of the modified portion.

The lower fuselage service areas, forward and aft of the wing junctions, were not pressurized and access to these places was via hinged doors located in the bottom centre-line of the aircraft. A majority of the hydraulic system units and a reserve oil tank were contained in the forward servicing area, while the aileron booster unit, wing flap and aileron actuating devices and the ground/air-conditioning connection were housed in the rear servicing area.

Accommodation aboard the L-1649A was similar to that of the Super-G Constellation. The flight deck housed the captain, first officer, radio operator and flight engineer. Aft of them, the navigator sat on the port side of a small compartment, in which the opposite side was a crew rest area. The entrance for the crew was via a starboard door, which provided direct access to the flight deck. Immediately aft of the navigator's position and crew rest area was the forward passenger cabin, a central door in the cabin bulkhead providing access from the flight deck area to the front passenger compartment. Port and starboard toilets, with wardrobes, were located at the rear of the forward cabin. An aisle led between the toilets to the main passenger cabin, where a sloping floor led to the after end of this compartment. Another doorway through a bulkhead provided access to a lounge area, while the next bulkhead to the rear allowed access to the

Contemporaries of the Super Constellation and Starliner on Lockheed's production lines were the P2V Neptune, F-94C Starfire, T-33A and the famous C-130 transport. This fine air-to-air photo shows a P2V-7 of the US Navy in overall dark blue finish.

An USAF Lockheed T-33A (16624) in transit at a USAF base in Japan during the Korean War.

same lounge from the passenger entrance lobby. Once the aircraft was ready for take-off, the main door to this lobby was locked by multiple bolts, linked to a single handle. Behind the rear bulkhead of the entrance lobby was the rearmost passenger cabin, followed by wardrobes, washrooms and, finally, the port and starboard toilets, which were located immediately in front of the fuselage production break-line.

A galley, on the starboard side of the aircraft, was situated opposite the main passenger entry door and provided hot and cold meals served by the cabin staff. Coffee, preheated before a flight, was kept in insulated containers in the galley and served piping hot. Folding seats, provided for the convenience of the cabin staff, were located in a small area aft of the rearmost passenger cabin. A useful 593cu.ft of cargo space was divided between a forward and rear freight and baggage hold, incorporated into the lower fuselage beneath the front and rear passenger compartments.

The L-1649A was equipped with a marker beacon, twin ADF loops, a radar safety beacon (FF), radio and altimeter antennae and the ADF sense aerial, all fitted in the under-belly area, ahead of the centre-section. Located in the flight deck roof was a VOR antenna and HF radio aerial, the mast for which was equipped with a de-icing boot, while a VHF antenna was fitted in a dorsal position.

Like its predecessor, Lockheed's L-1649A Starliner featured pneumatically-operated de-icer boots, fitted integrally to all leading edges, including the triple fins. The wing leading and trailing edges and tips were no-step areas for service and maintenance purposes, the servicing points being accessible from the centre portions of the wing. Four fuel-filling positions were located on the top of the starboard wing and three on the port wing. Engine oil was replenished via fillers in the top of each power-plant.

Evolved from the T-33 two-seat trainer, the Lockheed F-94 Starfire was designed as a two-seat all-weather interceptor equipped with radar equipment. This was an early F-94A variant with a 6,000lb thrust Allison J-33-A-33 and four-gun armament in the forward fuselage. Note: wingtip tanks fitted beneath the wings. USAF serial 49-2503 (Buzz No FA-503).

Each engine contained a 45 gallon (US) oil tank, the recommended grade of oil being 120 (Wright Aero Division Specification 5815). Fillers for the alcohol used in the anti-icing system were situated on top of the outboard engines, aft of the oil filter location, to the rear of the nacelle where there was an anti-icing service area. Each of the two alcohol tanks had a capacity of 20 gallons (US).

When construction of the L-1649A commenced, Lockheed's Burbank plant had expanded to occupy an area of 2million sq.ft, much of which involved Super Constellation and, subsequently, Starliner production. However, this space also included indirect facilities, such as administration, tooling, engineering and general services, which were also applied to other contemporary Lockheed aircraft types being produced including the P2V Neptune anti-submarine patrol bomber, the T-33 jet-trainer, F94C Starfire fighter and the C-130 Hercules transport. Space directly involving Super Constellation production, including the military R7V-Is, WV-2s and RC-121Cs, amounted to 700,000sq.ft for assembly lines, and 250,000sq.ft for the fabrication of components exclusively for the Super Constellations. These facilities were envisaged as being readily available for L-1649A Starliner production, although Lockheed's California Division also included factories at Bakersfield, Palmdale, Beverly Hills and Van Nuys. The Division's tot`al floor space was 5,976,000sq.ft. There was another plant at Marietta, Georgia, with 4,455,000sq.ft of floor space, but this was given over to production of

The Super Constellation's other Lockheed production line contemporary was the famous C-130 Hercules transport, used widely in many countries in both a military and civil role. This civil variant (A2-ACA) is seen during the 1970s in Air Botswana Cargo service.

Lockheed's C-130 Hercules turboprop transport and Boeing B-47 Stratojet bombers, produced under contract.

Lockheed ran two training-schools, intended especially for the use of civil and military operators of the Constellation family and the Starliner. One school devoted itself to Flight Operations, the other functioning as a Service Group. The Flight Operations unit concentrated on instructing pilots and flight engineers on specific features of the aircraft, the plan being that optimum performance would be gained by the civil or military operator from the aircraft's delivery date. The Service Group specialized in familiarizing customers' personnel with maintenance procedures and techniques on Lockheed's latest airliner models. One example was a course entitled 'Line Maintenance', the curriculum covering the entire aircraft. Both groups used actual Super Constellations or L-1649As in various stages of construction for familiarization, while numbers of components were made up as operating models, including panels, gauges, levers and controls.

Lockheed strategically stationed company specialists in those parts of the world where the Constellations and Starliners operated in order that they would be available to assist the airline operators themselves. Thus, by making periodic visits these Lockheed field representatives were able to liaise between their company and the airline operators on matters regarding maintenance and engineering. Wherever an airline customer was introducing the Constellation or Starliner into service, a Lockheed special representative was assigned to that airline for a period.

Banking to port is the prototype L-1649 (c/n 1001), its first flight taking place on 11 October 1956. Registered N 1649 this aircraft entered TWA service on 1 June 1957.

On 11 October 1956 the prototype Starliner, N1649, took off from Burbank on its maiden flight. With R. Wimmer and H.R. Salmon heading the test crew, the trip proved uneventful, with no problems. This was followed by a series of test flights, during which N1649 undertook in excess of 100 trips across the blue waters of the Pacific Ocean. This programme of tests proved, without any shadow of doubt, the advantages of the new laminar flow wing, the uprated engines, redesigned functional systems and the larger, slower-turning, three-blade propellers. It was obvious the L-1649A Shrliner had reached a pinnacle in piston-engine, passenger-carrying, aircraft development, introducing new standards of comfort, performance and dependability in aircraft of that category. Accommodation was initially for fifty-eight first-class passengers (later sixty-two), or seventy-five tourist-class passengers (later ninety-two and, eventually, ninety-nine).

As with earlier Constellations, TWA was the first to purchase a production L-1649A Starliner, which they promptly designated their 'Jetstream' Class. The first machine to enter TWA service was cn.1002. This aircraft had first been used in the type's certification programme, which was successfully concluded and approved on 27 March 1957. After delivery to TWA it was registered as N7301 C, given the

The second Starliner built was c/n 1002, seen here in its smart TWA livery. As can be seen, none of the beautiful lines of the original series of Connies and Super Connies has been sacrificed.

company fleet number 301, and named *Star of Wyoming*. The Starliner's excellent range made it suitable for TWA's North Atlantic route and, on 1 June 1957, the airline commenced its New York-London-Paris service, with Frankfurt being added just one month later. On 30 September of that year, TWA inaugurated their new service from San Francisco, on the west coast of America, to London, a distance of 5,500 miles, which was covered in just over $18\frac{1}{2}$ hours. Because of its new wing, the Starliner was able to accomplish other record flights. For example, a Burbank to Paris run was made in sixteen hours and twenty-one minutes, while similar flights from Burbank were made to Hamburg, and London. Another L-1649A flight was made non-stop between New York and Athens. As well as TWA, Lockheed Starliners were used by Air France, Condor Flugdienst, Lufthansa, Trek Airways and World Airways. Potential for a long production-run of the Lockheed L-1649A Starliner looked promising but, unfortunately, the type arrived too late. The big jet-engine Boeing 707s and Douglas DC-8s were entering service world-wide, in ever increasing numbers. It was apparent that the days of the large piston-engine airliners were numbered, as far as the major operators were concerned. The end of an era was fast approaching, which had, in its day, been on a par with the earlier, golden age of flying-boats.

The death knell for the Starliner as a major passenger transport was sounded by a new generation of jetliners, like this Douglas DC-8 of Delta Airlines, with four 18,000lb thrust Pratt & Whitney JT-3D-3 turbofans. It cruised at 579mph at 30,000ft, had a five-man crew and carried up to 189 passengers.

Relegated to secondary routes and companies, the Starliner flew on for a number of years. This machine (N7316C), initially with TWA, went to Alaska Airlines; was later with the Prudhoe Bay Oil Distributing Co, Alaska. It then moved to West Air Inc., of Bethel, Alaska, and eventually passed to Burns Aviation Inc., (USA). It is seen here still operating in 1969.

9 The Constellation Family and Major Airlines

Before the advent of the Second World War, TWA only flew US domestic routes but, after 5 July 1945, the company broadened its horizons with two international routes, granted by the Civil Aeronautics Bureau. Operating from the major US cities of Boston, Chicago, Detroit, New York and Philadelphia, the new services would be able to fly to Europe and beyond, with the first stop at Gander, Newfoundland, for refuelling. From there, a scheduled northern or southern route was to operate across the Atlantic to Cairo, Egypt, and eventually India. The northern route included a refuelling stop in Ireland, before continuing to Paris, Geneva, Rome, Athens and Cairo. The southern service flew via Lisbon, Algiers, Tunis, Tripoli and Benghazi, while a link service was provided between the two routes, which operated from Lisbon to Rome, via Madrid. Later, TWA commenced a service from Cairo to Bombay, this flying via Tel Aviv, Basra and Dhahran.

TWA's first international service was inaugurated on 5 February 1946, when Lockheed L-049 Constellation, N86511, *Star of Paris* (cn.2035), left La Guardia Airport, New York, for Paris. On board were thirty-six passengers, a crew of eight and some cargo. Refuelling stops were made at Gander and Shannon. The flight was completed in nineteen hours and forty-six minutes. On that occasion the pilot was TWA's Capt. Harold F. Blackburn. The aircraft was one of twenty-seven L-049s ordered by TWA shortly after the end of the war with Japan. Due to the airline's great help in developing the Constellation, it was given priority in delivery of the new airliners and guaranteed the first L-049s from Lockheed would fly with TWA. Indeed, the first new Constellation arrived with the company on 15 November 1946 and TWA had taken delivery of a further nine L-049s by the end of the year.

The day before TWA's inaugural New York to Paris flight, the president of the airline, Jack Frye, flew a Constellation from Burbank, California, to La Guardia airport, New York in a record time of seven hours and twenty-eight minutes. Ten days later, on 15 February 1946, Howard Hughes piloted L-049 *Star of California*, from Los Angeles to New York, in eight hours and thirty-eight minutes. This flight actually inaugurated TWA's American coast-to-coast service with Constellations. On the same day the airline commenced its scheduled service to Rome, via Gander, Shannon and Paris. The aircraft doing the honours on that occasion was L-049 (cn.2034), NC86510, *Star of Rome*.

Ironically, for its inaugural service to Cairo on 1 April 1946, TWA used a Douglas DC-4 Skymaster, named *Acropolis*, which flew from Washington DC, to Egypt, via New York, Gander, Shannon, Paris, Rome and Athens. In just under twenty-nine hours the DC-4 had landed at Payne Field, Cairo (now Cairo International Airport). The following month, on 3 May, TWA introduced the L-049 Constellation as the

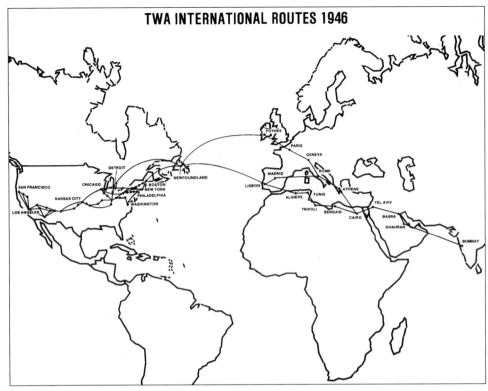

TWA INTERNATIONAL ROUTES 1946

The international route map of TWA in 1946, flown mainly by the airline's Lockheed Constellation fleet.

only type on its Egyptian route, starting from Chicago, and flying to Cairo, via New York, Gander, Shannon and European cities.

TWA's last L-049 Constellation delivery came off Lockheed's production line during 1946, this being cn.2088, civil registration N90826, fleet number 515, named *Star of the China Sea*. Because of an airline pilots' strike in October 1947, TWA cancelled eight of the L-049s it had ordered but, even worse for Lockheed, a contract worth $20million, involving eighteen model L-649 Constellations, was cancelled. However, a year later, TWA introduced an all-sleeper Constellation service on its New York to Paris service. Also, in 1950 (the year that DC-4s were phased out on TWA's international routes) the old name, Transcontinental and Western Air was dropped, in favour of Trans World Airways, thus retaining the old TWA initials. In its Lockheed Constellations TWA had a pressurized aircraft on its transatlantic services, capable of carrying up to forty-seven passengers at a cruising speed of 270mph. This provided a faster, higher and more comfortable flight than that of the earlier DC-4 service. In 1952 TWA's Constellations were modified to accommodate up to sixty passengers, which enabled the company to inaugurate its transatlantic 'Sky Tourist' service for 'coach'-class passengers.

On 23 October 1945, Pan American Airways (which became Pan American World Airways in 1950) had ordered twenty-two Lockheed Model L-049 Constellations

On 5 February 1946, TWA's L-049 Constellation, NC86511 Star of Paris, fleet No 555, prepares to depart from New York's LaGuardia Airport on the airline's inaugural flight to Paris. It carried thirty-six passengers, a crew of eight and some cargo. The flight took almost twenty hours, including refuelling stops at Gander and Shannon.

TWA used a Douglas DC-4 to inaugurate its USA (Washington DC) to Egypt (Cairo) service on 1 April 1946, via New York, Gander, Shannon, Paris, Rome and Athens. Named Acropolis *the DC-4 is seen here after arrival at Payne Field (later Cairo International Airport). A month later TWA replaced its DC-4s on this USA to Egypt route with Lockheed Constellations starting from Chicago.*

and the first aircraft, N88831 (cn.2031), was delivered to the airline on 5 January 1946. On 3 February 1946 Pan American (PanAm) introduced Constellations on their New York to Bermuda service, and by the end of 1949, L-049s had replaced the Boeing Model 314A Yankee Clipper flying-boats on PanAm's San Francisco and Honolulu service. L-049s were soon operating PanAm's route to Natal, Brazil, Lisbon, Dakar, Monrovia and Leopoldville, in the Belgian Congo. The company had already established itself on the North Atlantic route with L-049s, starting in February 1946, when La Guardia airport, New York, was linked with the UK (at Hum Airport), via Gander and Shannon.

In South America, Panair do Brasil, a subsidiary of PanAm, was supplied with three Lockheed L-049 Constellations by the parent company. The first of these was delivered, to Rio de Janeiro, on 31 March 1946. This aircraft (cn.2049) was initially registered as N88849, but later received the Brazilian registration PP-PCF, and was named *Manoel de Borba Gato*. It undertook a proving flight from Rio to London, via Recife and Dakar, on 16 April 1946, and, on landing at London's new Heathrow Airport, was the first aircraft from a foreign airline to do so. The first scheduled Constellation service to London from Rio de Janeiro, by Panair do Brasil, commenced on 27 April 1946. That same year, as more new Constellations were delivered to the airline, the Rio to Europe routes were extended to Paris, on 1 July, and Rome, on 3 October. During 1947 Panair do Brasil's services expanded, to include Cairo from 5 June and Istanbul from 16 November, while on 9 March 1948 the Paris route was extended to Frankfurt, West Germany.

From early 1946 until the mid-1950s, Lockheed's Model L-049 and L-149 Constellation became Panair do Brasil's flagships. By the end of April 1949 these types had completed more than 1,000 crossings of the South Atlantic. Furthermore, on 5 October 1949 the Istanbul service was extended to Beirut, and, in 1951, Panair do Brasil's South American network, which already included Montevideo and Buenos

An L-749 Constellation (NC91207) ex-works with the type name emblazoned along the fuselage. This machine later went to TWA as N91207 with the fleet No 707.

Aires, added Santiago, Chile, and Lima, the capital of Peru, to its routes. On 30 December 1953, one of Panair do Brasil's Constellations claimed a record, flying non-stop from Lisbon to Rio de Janeiro, a distance of 4,837 miles, in twenty-one hours and forty minutes. Earlier in 1953, this airline had added Hamburg to its list of European destinations and, on 22 March 1954, a service to Dusseldorf was included.

In the UK, BOAC had faced a dilemma in 1946, for it was intending to introduce a new and suitable aircraft, of British origin, to its fleet, specifically for the North Atlantic route. It chose the Avro Tudor Mk1, a pressurized design, powered by four Rolls-Royce Merlin 621 engines. However, the Tudor 1 was built to carry only twelve passengers and, despite a lengthy gestation period, was still presenting a number of aerodynamic problems. Matters worsened when, at a meeting held on 12 March 1946, BOAC stipulated over 340 modifications they would require. Just over a year later, on 11 April 1947, the Tudor contract was cancelled.

No other British airliner design was immediately available at that time (the Handley Page Hermes was nearly four years away) and BOAC had no other choice but to place an order with Lockheed for eight L-049 Constellations. The first machine (cn.1975) was registered G-AHEJ, named *Bristol II*, and introduced on BOAC's New York to London service, via Gander and Shannon. When first entering service BOAC Constellations were, basically, in an overall metal finish, this being replaced later by the well-known white fuselage top, carrying the black letters 'BOAC' each side and a black cheat line. The famous Speedbird emblem was applied to the outer rudders, with the individual aircraft registration beneath it. Each BOAC Constellation was allotted a name, which was painted in white, beneath the cockpit,

The L-049 Constellation flew with Pan American Airways, the type first entering service on the airline's New York to Bermuda route on 3 February 1946. This particular L-049 is N88832 and simply named Clipper.

By 1949 Lockheed Constellations had ousted the famous Boeing 314A Yankee Clipper flying boats on Pan American Airways San Francisco to Honolulu route. This was one of these flying boats, NC 18603. Note the name Yankee Clipper *on the side.*

on each side. A typical example was G-AHEM (cn.1978), named *Balmoral*. Later, between 1948 and 1955, BOAC acquired a further seventeen Lockheed Constellations, these being the modified L-749A version.

QANTAS was another airline with great faith in the capabilities of the Constellation, for in October 1946, QANTAS signed a contract for the delivery of four new L-749 Constellations, at a total cost of $5.5 million. On their arrival a year later, the four machines were prepared for a weekly service on the original 'Kangaroo' route to London, via Singapore, this having re-opened eighteen months earlier, in April 1946. It was at about this time that QANTAS became entirely Australian-owned. The old Imperial Airways half-share had been acquired from that airline's successor, BOAC, by the Australian Government which, on 3 July 1947, bought up the remaining local shareholding, making QANTAS Australia's national overseas air service. Five months later, on 1 December 1947, the first QANTAS Constellation, VH-EAA, (cn.2562), named *Ross Smith*, took off from Kingsford Smith Airport, Sydney, on the first leg of its flight to London. The flight introduced the first QANTAS stewardess service.

This Constellation, VH-EAA, *Ross Smith*, had created much enthusiasm and excitement when it arrived on its delivery flight from Lockheed. This flight was made in the record time thirty-three hours in flight, from a total elapsed journey time of forty-three hours. Waiting to greet the aircraft and its crew were: the Australian Minister for Air, Mr Drakeford; Mr Hudson Fysh, chairman and managing director of QANTAS and Sir Keith Smith who, with his brother Ross, had made the first flight between England and Australia in 1919, flying a converted Vickers Vimy bomber.

Those present to welcome this graceful new airliner were truly amazed to see it reverse into position in front of the Kingsford Smith terminal building. It was the

A Lockheed L-749A Constellation, N90926, on a wet day at London Airport in the early style Pan Am colour scheme.

first aircraft in Australia to feature reversible pitch propellers. Pressurization was also something new in a passenger aircraft in Australia, as was the 'floating' cabin, referred to by one reporter as a cabin within a cabin, in which the entire wall of the of the passenger section floats free of the main aircraft structure on a bed of rubber. Norman Ellison, an aviation writer, described the Constellation in the *Sydney Sun*, stating, 'The Constellations have more new features than any other airliner in a decade. They add up to greater speed, a higher degree of safety, more comfort, and bigger and better menus'. With the latter, of course, came the newly introduced stewardesses, or as they became popularly known, air hostesses.

Australia had been virtually isolated during the Second World War but, in 1952, a new fortnightly service was inaugurated between Sydney and Johannesburg, South Africa, providing Australia a second strategic route to the UK. The coronation of Her Majesty Queen Elizabeth II took place in 1953, and to honour this great occasion all QANTAS Constellations on the Sydney to London route proudly carried the Coronation crest and conveyed special Coronation airmail souvenirs. Further honours befell QANTAS in 1954 when Her Majesty the Queen visited Australia. Together with HRH the Duke of Edinburgh, Her Majesty was flown on her Australian tour in the L-749 Constellation VH-EAF (cn.2504), named *Horace Brinsmead*, after the first controller of Civil Aviation in Australia. During the Royal tour, an original pioneer of QANTAS, Hudson Fysh, was made a Knight of the British Empire in a ceremony at Government House, Sydney. This was the first investiture made by a British Sovereign in Australia.

In 1951, QANTAS had ordered three new Super Constellations. After their arrival, in 1954, operations began across the Pacific on 15 May, with a twice-weekly service operating from Sydney, via Fiji, Canton Island and Hawaii. One service

Britain's ill-fated Avro Tudor airliner forced BOAC to purchase Lockheed Constellations as no other suitable British design was then available. This shot is of a Tudor (G-AHKN) operated by British South African Airways (BSAA).

One of the BOAC Constellations as G-AHEM Balmoral. It was originally No 42-94557, USAAF. In June 1955 this machine went to the USA as N2735A of Capital Airlines.

terminated at San Francisco, the other at Vancouver, Canada. Further orders for Super Constellations were placed by QANTAS. When Australia played host to the XVIth Olympic Games at Melbourne, in 1956, QANTAS carried record traffic on all its routes. In addition to scheduled services, no less than seventy special Olympic Games flights were undertaken. During that time QANTAS had its entire Super Constellation fleet in the air at the same time on at least a dozen occasions, a fitting tribute to both the aircraft and QANTAS engineering and maintenance staff. The airline also flew the Olympic Flame in a Super Constellation, from Athens to Darwin, a flight of some 8,600 miles, the longest journey ever made with the Flame and the first time it had crossed the Equator to the Southern Hemisphere.

In 1957 an important agreement was made between Australia and the US, when permission was granted for QANTAS to operate across the US, via San Francisco and New York, before flying on across the Atlantic, to the UK and Europe. This enabled QANTAS to begin operating its round-the-world service, the first of its kind, which was inaugurated on 14 January 1958, with two Lockheed Super-G Constellations, VH-EAO (cn.4679), named *Southern Aurora*, and VH-EAP (cn.4680), named *Southern Zephyr*. The two aircraft left Melbourne for Sydney, where they parted company, with one heading west along the 'Kangaroo' route, to London via the Middle East, while the second Super-G flew east across the Pacific to San Francisco, New York and on to London. Soon eight round-the-world services per week were operating, four by QANTAS, and four in association with BOAC. As a point of interest Super-G, VH-EAO (acquired on 28 October 1957) returned to Lockheed on 14 October 1959, becoming N9722C, but within a year (on 18 August 1960) was sent back to QANTAS reregistered as VH-EAO, whereupon it was renamed, appropriately, *Southern Prodigal*. This aircraft then remained with QANTAS for almost three years before being sold to Calif Airmotive, an American owned airline.

After serving with BOAC and Ace Freighters, this L-749A was sold to Euravia as seen here. Later it went to Aerolineas Uruguayas as CX-BHC.

An L-749 Constellation, VH-EAC, of Australia's airline QANTAS, being serviced at London Airport (Heathrow) in the 1950s.

Thanks to Super Constellations, QANTAS and the flying kangaroo emblem became a familiar sight in twenty-three countries, on five continents, around the world. By the end of 1958 QANTAS had extended its international network to 72,725 miles. Only one QANTAS Super Constellation was involved in an accident. This was VH-EAM (cn.4606), *Southern Wave*, which crashed on 24 August 1960 while taking off from Mauritius. Fortunately there were no fatal casualties but the aircraft was damaged beyond repair. Two QANTAS Super Constellations were L-1049H dual-purpose variants, used as passenger and cargo aircraft. The first one, VH-EAM (cn.4801), *Southern Spray*, was the subject of a special christening ceremony, in October 1956, to celebrate the type's dual role. This occasion was intended to highlight the L-1049H variants purpose as a passenger and cargo carrying aircraft. Two Australian women, Lola Fry and Pamela Cooke, stood, one each side of the Super H's nose, on raised platforms, each breaking a traditional bottle of champagne on the port and starboard sides. During 1956 the two L-1049Hs entered service to assist with the QANTAS Pacific runs involved with the Olympic Games traffic.

When Boeing 707 jets began entering QANTAS service, the airline's Super Constellations were relegated to mundane duties like freighting, but this too lessened as extra cargo space became available on the big jets. Nevertheless, in 1959 the two QANTAS L-1049Hs participated in a massive airlift, transporting 46,000lb of components between the US and Australia to construct a Boeing simulator, which QANTAS acquired from the American company.

Meanwhile, although early variants of the Constellation continued to provide an excellent service with various airlines, in both the passenger and cargo-carrying role, it was not long before they were joined by L-1049 Super Constellations and subsequent variants. As they had with the original Constellation programme, TWA gave their full support to development of the Super Constellation series. However, they were the second airline to receive the new version. EAL beat them to it, with the first delivery of fourteen L-1049s ordered arriving in time to enter the type on its scheduled New York to Miami service on 15 December 1951. These fourteen Super Constellations (cns 4001-4014) were registered N6201C-N6214C, *en-bloc*, and given EAL fleet numbers 201-214. At the beginning of 1958 EAL possessed a total 187 piston-engine airliners in its fleet, for operating both short and long-haul routes. These aircraft included fifty-six Lockheed Constellations and Super Constellations, of which forty-six were various versions of the Super Constellation. Other types included seven Douglas DC-6Bs, 48 DC-7Bs, twenty Convair CV-440s and fifty-six Martin 4-0-4s. In April 1961, EAL inaugurated the world's first guaranteed-seat service, with no reservations required, this 'air shuttle' starting with the airline's Super Constellations.

Of the twenty-four L-1049s built, the remaining ten went to TWA, which commenced its New York to Los Angeles service on 10 September 1952. The ten machines (cns 4015-4024) were registered N6901C-N6910C, *en-bloc*, and given TWA fleet numbers 901-910. After the updated L-1049C Super Constellation was introduced, the prototype of which first flew on 17 February 1953, those airlines ordering this variant were assured of an improved performance in comparison to the L-1049 model. This was due to the installation of more powerful Wright Turbo-Compound engines and a higher take-off weight. The first L-1049C (cn.4501) was delivered to KLM on 10 June 1953 and registered PH-TFP. On 15 August of that year, this machine entered service on KLM's non-stop New York to Amsterdam

Another QANTAS L-749A Constellation, VH-EAE, pictured at London Heathrow in the 1950s.

Super Constellation L- 1049G, VH-EAD Southern Dawn, *in its element with a seascape backdrop. Note the airline's name on the tip tanks.*

Eventually QANTAS sold off its Super Constellations as a new generation of Boeing 707 Jetliners replaced them. Here a QANTAS Boeing 707, VH-EBO, prepares for a night flight.

route, although on the return trip a refuelling stop was made at either Prestwick or Shannon. This was normal procedure for westbound transatlantic airliners in those days, because of the prevailing Atlantic headwinds that were usually encountered. Other KLM long-haul routes included Australia, South Africa and South America. To operate them KLM acquired a further twelve L-1049Cs for its fleet. The first eight machines were initially registered PH-TFR, PH-TFS, PH-TFT, PH-TFU, PH-TFV, PH-TFW, PH-TFX and PH-TFY (cns 4502-4509, respectively). Later these registrations were changed to PH-LKR, PH-LKS, PH-LKT, PH-LKU, PH-LKV, PH-LKW, PH-LKX and PH-LKY respectively, while the original PH-TFP became PH-LKP. The remaining four L-1049Cs were delivered as PH-LKA, PH-LKB, PH-LKC, and PH-LKD (cns 4553, 4558, 4559 and 4560 respectively).

TWA put its L-1049C Constellations into service on its Ambassador route, between Los Angeles and New York, on 19 October 1953, this being the first regular, scheduled, non-stop, transcontinental service operated on a coast-to-coast basis. Seven L-1049Cs, from the last eleven built, were delivered to TWA (cns 4550, 4551, 4552, 4554, 4555, 4557 and 4558). The other four went to KLM, including cn.4560, which was the final L-1049C produced before construction of the first L-1049E (cn.4561) commenced, although most 'E' models emerged off the assembly lines as L-1049Gs.

First in the L-1049 Super Constellation series, N6201 C, which after its initial flight trials in August 1951 entered service with Eastern Air Lines on 15 December that year.

L-1049H, PH-LKL, of the Dutch airline KLM, is shown in landing mode. The size of the lowered flaps and the tip tanks that were fitted can be seen.

Adding to its fleet of seventeen L-1049s and L-1049Cs, TWA purchased thirty-eight more Super Constellations, including twenty-nine of the more advanced L-1049G Super-G model and nine L-1049Hs, the dual-purpose passenger/freight variant. It was during 1956 that its Super Constellations enabled TWA to inaugurate a transatlantic, two-class passenger service (first-class and tourist). In the following year transpolar routes were opened by TWA, between Los Angeles and London via San Francisco, and to Paris and Rome.

The L-1049C production programme was intended primarily to supply TWA and KLM with the type but other international airlines began sending in orders and, in the event, sixty L-1049Cs were built. Of these, in addition to the thirteen and seven delivered to KLM and TWA respectively, ten went to Air France (cns 4510-4519), with registrations F-BGNA, F-BGNB, F-BGNC, F-BGND, F-BGNE, F-BGNF, F-BGNG, F-BGNH, F-BGNI, and F-BGNJ. Another two went to Air India (cns 4547 and 4548) as VT-DGL and VT-DGM, and sixteen went to EAL (cns 4523-4538), registered N6215C to N6230C respectively, the EAL fleet numbers also corresponded accordingly, from 215 to 230. Another three L-1049Cs flew with Pakistan International Airlines (cns 4520, 4521 and 4522), registered as AP-AFQ, AP-AFR and AP-AFS. QANTAS received its four L-1049Cs (cns 4539, 4545, 4546 and 4549) as VH-EAG, VH-EAH, VH-EAI and VH-EAJ, while Trans Canada Airlines (TCA), received five L-1049Cs (cns 4540, 4541, 4542, 4543 and 4544) as CF-TGA, CF-TGB, CF-TGC, CF-TGD and CF-TGE, with fleet numbers 401, 402, 403, 404 and 405. As with earlier Constellations, quite a number of the Super Constellations changed hands as more modern types of aircraft entered service with major airlines and, consequently, several construction numbers and registrations can be found in the colours of a number of secondary airlines.

Air France, which had formed in August 1933 with the merger of four airlines Air Union, Farman, CIDNA, and Air Orient had expanded rapidly before the Second World War erupted. During the war, those machines that could be salvaged from the Air France fleet went to North Africa in support of the Allies. Then, on 26 June 1945, the French civil aviation industry was nationalized and Air France changed its status from a private company to a state enterprise. Expansion soon followed and much-needed new equipment, like Lockheed Constellations and Super Constellations, began arriving to supplement the airline's DC-3s and DC-4s. By 1950 Air France was carrying treble the number of passengers carried by French airlines during the twenty-year period before the war. On 20 October 1950 they inaugurated a service to Montreal, Canada. The company's first service to Mexico started less than two years later, on 27 April 1952. By 1954 the Air France fleet included twenty-one L-749 and 749A Constellations and ten Super Constellations, as well as other types. These Constellation variants enabled the airline to further develop its international routes. On 10 April 1958, Air France began flying the polar route to Japan and China, via Anchorage, Alaska, and a Moscow service was inaugurated in that August.

On 6 May 1959 the French-built Caravelle jet airliner was introduced on Air France's Paris to Istanbul service, via Rome and Athens. At the time the French airline's fleet was still made up mostly of Lockheed types including fifteen Constellations, twenty-two Super Constellations and ten of the L-1649A Starliners. However, by the early part of 1960, Boeing 707 jets were joining the Air France fleet and four decades of French, piston-engine, civil airliners began drawing to a close. Most of the Lockheed machines were disposed of, although when Max Bruch was

A L-1049G, N7106C, in TWA service during 1956. Note the TWA logo painted on the tip tanks.

This L-1049 Super Connie is pictured in the 1960s when operating with Pakistan International Airways as AP-AJZ. Note the tail markings.

Air France's manager in the Far East, during the early 1960s, the airline's Super-G Constellations were operating the Paris to the Far East service four times a week. After their order for L-749As, Air France had contracted for fourteen Super-Gs (cns 4620-4727, 4634 and 4639), registrations F-BHBA through to F-BHBJ, and (cns 4668-4671) F-BHMI through to F-HBML.

As previously noted, Air India had received two L-1049C Super Constellations and an order for a further eight was placed with Lockheed. These arrived in Bombay as three Model L-1049Es (cns 4613-4615), VT-DHL, VT-DHM and VT-DHN, and five L-1049Gs (cns 4646, 4666, 4667, 4686 and 4687), VT-DIL, VT-DIM, VT-DIN, VT-DJW and VT-DIX.

Air India International had become the state-owned Air India on 8 June 1962. The airline's Super Constellations enabled it to open new routes in an easterly direction, taking in Singapore (via Madras), Bangkok, Hong Kong, Tokyo, Darwin and Sydney. From April 1959 Air India was able to add Tashkent and Moscow to its list of destinations, by which time the airline had increased its route lengths to 19,000 miles.

Pakistan International Airlines Corporation (PIA) started using its first three L-1049C Super Constellations on 7 June 1954, flying the route between Karachi, West Pakistan, and Dacca, East Pakistan (now Bangladesh). However, PIA really came into its own after 11 March 1955, when it merged with Orient Airways Ltd, which had been the major domestic operator within Pakistan until then. Thus, PIA now became an autonomous corporation, which, as well as serving East and West Pakistan, flew to the Middle East, India, Burma and Europe. For these services, in addition to its L-1049Cs, Vickers Viscounts and DC-3s, PIA acquired two more Super Constellations, these being the L-1049H convertible passenger/cargo variety (cns 4835 and 48360), registered AP-AJY and AP-AJZ.

Success of earlier variants of the Super Constellation persuaded well over a dozen of the world's major airlines to choose the Super-G model as it became available. Another airline loyal to Lockheed's Super Constellation family was Trans-Canada Air Lines (TCA), which added another nine of the type to those five L-1049Cs already in service (mentioned earlier). These nine consisted of: three L-1049Es (cns 4563, 4564 and 4565), registered CF-TGF, CF-TGG and CF-TGH; four L-1049G Super-Gs (cns 4641, 4643, 4682 and 4683), registered CF-TEU, CF-TEV, CF-TEW and CF-TEX and two L-1049Hs (cns 4850 and 4851), CF-TEY and CF-TEZ. These aircraft, together with the original five L-1049Cs, were employed from 14 May 1954, on TCA's transatlantic routes. From the following 26 September, the Super Constellations replaced TCA's Canadiar North Stars on Canadian transcontinental services. By the end of 1957 TCA's Super-G Constellations were flying the airline's non-stop routes across the Atlantic, to London, Paris and Dusseldorf.

In West Germany, Deutsche Luft Hansa, had been forced to close down in 1945. It was re-formed as Luftag in 1953, changing its name to Deutsche Lufthansa AG on 6 August 1954, and awaited the arrival of its first four Lockheed L-1049G Super-G Constellations. These Super-Gs (cns 4602-4605), were registered D-ALAK, D-ALEM, D-ALIN and D-ALOP. They were soon employed on Lufthansa's Hamburg to New York service, via Dusseldorf and Shannon, beginning on 8 June 1955. More cities were added on the North Atlantic route, which

An early L-049 Constellation F-BAZB, flying over what is believed to be rather hostile Middle Eastern terrain.

119

An Air France L-1049G Super constellation, F-BHBI, in 1966. This aircraft later went to the French company Air Fret.

included a direct service between Manchester and Chicago, commencing on 23 April 1956. The following August a new route was opened between West Germany and Argentina (Buenos Aires), which was extended to Santiago during May 1958.

By then Lufthansa had ordered four more Super-G Constellations (cns 4637, 4640, 4642 and 4267), registered D-ALAP, D-ALEC, D-ALOF and D-ALID. These aircraft supplemented the original four on the airline's long-distance routes, which now included the Middle East (which commenced in September 1956). Later a service to Bangkok began, during November 1959. By that time four L-1649A Starliners had joined the Lufthansa fleet. It is understood that two L-1049Hs entered service but, as the only details for these are cns 4820 and 4817, with registrations N1880 and N6921C, it is most likely they were only leased for a period. Certainly, during 1962-1963, Lufthansa did lease some of its L-1049G Super-G constellations to the Italian airline Alitalia, which mostly operated on charter flights.

A number of Super Constellations were employed by the Spanish airline, Lineas Aereas de Espana SA (IBERIA). The first three L-1049Cs were acquired in 1954 (cns 4550-4552), with registrations EC-AIN, EC-AIO and EC-AIP, and fleet numbers 201-2033. These aircraft opened up IBERIA's service to New York in September of that year. Soon routes were being extended to cover several European countries, North and South America and Africa, which necessitated ordering more aircraft, in the form of one more L-1049C (cn.4553), EC-AQL, and five L-1049G Super-Gs (cns 4673, 4676, 4644, 4645 and 4678), EC-AMP, EC-AMQ, EC-AQM, EC-AQN and EC-ARN.

Running up its engines at London Heathrow in the 1950s is VT-CQP, an L-749 Constellation of Air India International named Malabar Princess.

About to touch down at London Heathrow is an L-1049C Super Connie of Trans-Canada Airlines (registration unknown).

An Air India L-1049C Super Constellation, VT-DGM, of Air India International, being serviced at London Heathrow.

Standing on a wet runway and receiving some attention is D-ALEM, a Super 'G' Constellation of Lufthansa, mid-1960s.

137 This L-1049C, EC-AIN, fleet number 201, was with the Spanish airline Iberia when this picture was taken in the 1960s.

10 Latin American Constellations and Secondary Routes

(Note: the term 'Latin America' is taken to include Mexico, Central America and the Caribbean, in this volume.)

When aircraft were introduced into the vast continent of South America, an air link provided the most practical form of transport between populated areas. Separated by huge stretches of jungle, mountain ranges and plains, many towns and villages could most easily be reached by air. In the early days when aircraft were powered by one or, perhaps, two engines, flying over such hostile terrain could be hazardous, even for the most experienced pilots. However, following the Second World War, when four-engine transport aircraft became available, much of South America's way of life was transformed. Greater numbers of people and larger quantities of freight could be flown between the spread-out communities and, perhaps more importantly, the way was clear for a fast and efficient means of international travel for South Americans. Also, a great increase in the volume of exports which could be conveyed, far more rapidly, was made possible. The new transports consisted mainly of Douglas DC-4s and Lockheed Constellations, many of which were destined to serve for two decades or more in Latin American countries

Aeronaves de Mexico, an airline that had formed in 1952 after the merger of a number of small airlines, which was, to become one of Mexico's two national air services, started a Mexico City to New York service with Constellations on 16 December 1975. Initially, they leased two L-049 Constellations (cns 2052 and 2059), XA-MAG and XA-MAH, from PanAm, for use on the New York route. A while later, in 1978, the company acquired a further four Constellations, all L-749As (cns 2619,2~620,2665,NA), registered XA-MEW, XA-MEU, XA-MEV and XA-MOA. The first machine, XA-MEW, was named *Acapulco*.

Further south, in Colombia, the well-established airline AVIANCA had started its first international service on 21 March 1946, with flights to Ecuador in DC-3s. On 22 January 1947 the airline's long-distance, non-stop service to Miami was inaugurated, flown by DC-4Ss. Two years later this route was extended to New York and, by 1950, AVIANCA had increased its network to include transatlantic services to Lisbon, Rome and Paris. After 1950 Lockheed Constellations joined the AVIANCA fleet, with six Model L-749As, making it possible to add Madrid, Hamburg and Frankfurt to the company's European destinations. Caracas, in Venezuela, and San Juan, in Puerto Rico, became intermediate stops in April 1954 and June 1957. On 1 June 1957 a new service commenced to the Peruvian capital of Lima. This route included a stop at Quito,

Ecuador. AVIANCA's L-749As (cns 2663, 2664, 2544, 2557, 2564 and 2645) were registered HK-162, HK-163, HK-650, HK-651, HK-652 and HK-653.

After the Cuban airline, Cubana, had gained its independence from Pan Am, it soon expanded its services to include Spain. It undertook a route to Madrid from Havana, via the Azores, which started in April 1948, using DC-4s. As traffic increased, and more routes were added, Cubana introduced three Lockheed L-049 Constellations to its fleet, with the intention of using them to operate a service between Havana and Mexico City, via Merida, Venezuela. Two of the L-049s (cns 2036 and 2061) were registered CU-T-547 (ex-Pan Am) and CU-T-532.

From 1948 the Mexican airline, Aerovias Guest, had flown a DC-4 service from Mexico City to Madrid, Spain, via Miami, Bermuda, the Azores and Lisbon. In 1951 the company closed its Spanish service in order to concentrate on increasing the traffic on its Miami route. This so-called 'Route of the Sun', between Mexico City and the Florida resort, proved so popular that Aerovias Guest replaced its slower, unpressurized DC-4s with Lockheed Model L-749 and L-749A Constellations, the first of which entered service during the second week of November 1955. A direct service to Panama was already operating and this route was extended to Caracas, Venezuela, in April 1958. The four Constellations involved were two L-749s (cns 2053/NA), XA-GOQ and XA-GOS (the first named *Veracruz*), and two L-749As (cns 2572 and 2573), XA-LIO and XA-LIP.

Fine air-to-air shot of Lockheed L-1049G, PP-VDE, of the Brazilian airline Varig. The aesthetic beauty of the Super Connie's design is evident in this picture, which also shows to advantage the de-icer boots fitted to the leading edges of the wings, three fins and horizontal tailplane.

Linea Aeropostal Venezolana (LAV) has been one of the most important airlines in Venezuela since its formation, in January 1935. After expansion, following the Second World War, the company was able to purchase a number of new aircraft types, including Lockheed Model L-049s and L-749s. These Constellations inaugurated LAV's new international routes from Caracas, Venezuela, to New York and Port of Spain, Trinidad. Later, in November 1953, the Constellations began operating LAV's new transatlantic services to Rome, Lisbon and Madrid. Although a service to Panama was also started, LAV, like Aerovias Guest, found the Miami route far more of a profitable venture than the New York run and consequently dropped the latter. One of LAV's L-049s (cn.2064), N90926, was initially owned by American Overseas Airlines (AOA), named *Chicago*, but AOA leased it to LAV and it eventually passed to Pan Am as their *Clipper Ocean Herald*. The other Constellations in LAV's fleet included two L-049s (cns 2081 and 2082), registered YV-C-AME and YV-C-AMI, named *Simon Bolivar* and *Francisca de Miranda*, with fleet numbers 302 and 301. During 1947, LAV added two L-749s to its fleet (cns 2560 and 21561), registrations YV-C-AMA and YC-C-AMU, they were named *Jose Marti* and *Antonio Jose de Sucre*.

From 1962 until 1980, when it ceased operations, the Dominican Republic's airline, Aerovias Quisqueyana, flew six Lockheed Constellations in the northern Caribbean area. This small fleet consisted of three L-049s and a trio of L-749As. The L-049s were: HI-260(cn.2070), originally PH-TAW of KLM and then TWA's

Taxiing past is an L-1049C Super Connie, N1005C, partly finished in the colours of Aer Lingus, the Irish international airline. An ex-Eastern Airlines machine, it had also flown with Cubana as CU-P-573 and later flew until the mid-1960s with Capitol Airways Inc. (USA).

Waiting its next turn of duty here is an L-749 Constellation, XA-GOQ, of the Mexican airline Aerovias Guest in the 1960s.

N6000C, *Star of Newfoundland*, N9414H, (cn.2075), originally F-BAZD of Air France, before going to TWA as *Star of Lebanon*; HI-270(cn.2085), previously with TWA as N90823, *Star of the Yellow Sea*. The three L-749As, all originally built for EAL as L-649s, but retrofitted to L-749A standards, were cns 2520, 2522, 2523, registered HI-140 (ex-EAL N103A), HI-207 (ex-EALN 105A) and HI- 129 (ex-EAL N 106A). Another airline in the Dominican Republic which operated Constellations around the Caribbean, was ARGO SA. Of its fleet, two were L-749As (cns 2607 and 2603), HI-328 and HI-393, both having been USAF C-121As, serial numbered 48-615 and 48-611.

COPISA (Compania Peruana Intemacional de Aviacion SA), an airline founded in Peru during 1964, which lasted only nine years, employed Lockheed L-749As on its Lima, Cali, in Colombia, Panama and Miami routes. A service to Iquitos, on the Amazon, was started in 1967, as well as one to Maracaibo, Venezuela, but COPISA was forced to suspend its services for three months that year, resuming them until the cessation of operations in 1973. L-749A Four Constellations are known to have operated with COPISA.

One was OB-R-819 (cn.2523), originally built as an L-649 for EAL, but retro-fitted to L-749 standard and used by Aerovias Quisqueyana; N1949 (cn.2565), initially with BOAC, as G-ANUR, then going to ACE Freighters, Skyways of London Ltd, QANTAS, as VH-EAB, and, in 1968, to Aerolineas Uruguayas, as CX-BHC. Another was OB-R-802 (cn.2566), originally G-ALAO, with BOAC, then sold to Aer Lingus, as EI-ADE, then to the US for Capitol Airlines (later Capitol International Airways) as N4902C. A third was OB-R-889 (cn.2627),

Resting between duties at Miami International Airport on 4 October 1980 is an L-749A, HI-328, of ARGO S.A., Dominican Republic. Note the large, partly-open freight door.

initially with Air France, as F-BAZN, then passed to Royal Air Moroc (RAM), as CN-CCP. A fourth was cn.2630, N 1939, initially with South African Airways (SAA) as ZS-DBS. Two other L-749As (cns 2548 and 2549) ordered by COPISA were not delivered.

In Peru's capital, Lima, a small airline was formed in 1963, known as Lineas Aereas Nacionales SA (LANSA). As well as operating services to other populated areas in Peru, the company initiated a series of special tourist flights to places of interest, such as the ruins at Chan-Chan and Iquitos, on the Amazon. LANSA included among its fleet three Lockheed L-749 Constellations, all ex-EAL aircraft (cns 2614, 2518 and 2534) whose original registrations were N117A, N101A and N113A. In LANSA service they were initially registered OB-WAA, OB-WAB and OB-WAC (fleet numbers 732, 733,740), however later re-registration resulted in them becoming OB-R-732, OB-R-733 and OB-R-740.

As well as Pan Air do Brasil and those more prominent South American airlines included so far in this chapter, there were numerous other small, less well-known operators of first generation Lockheed Constellations in the Latin American area. A brief summary of some of these concerns follows. Aerolineas Carreras Transportes Aereos, of Argentina, flew L-749A LV-PBH (cn.2619), later re-registered LV-IIC. Aerolineas Uruguayas flew L-749A CX-BHC (cn.2565), (the company also had an option on L-749A (cn.2548), CX-BHD, which was not proceeded with). Aerotransportes Entre Rios SRL, of

After serving with Seaboard & Western (leased to Eastern Air Lines and Aer Lingus), with Cubana as CU-P-573 and Intercontinental US Inc., this L-1049C is seen in 1967 when operating with Capitol Airways as N 1005C.

Seen in 1969, after being withdrawn from use following service with Trans Peruana of Peru, is an L-749A Constellation registered OB-R-802. Judging by the appearance of this aircraft, it has probably been cannibalised to provide spares for other Connies.

Argentina, flew L-749A LV-PZX (cn.2540), (later re-registered as LV-IGS. Air Haiti International, flew an L-749A (cn.2615) which was lost at sea in November 1961. Brazilian operator Arruda flew L-049 PP-PDG (cn.2037), from 1971 until the aircraft crashed in May 1972. Between 1962 and 1967 CAUSA, of Uruguay, operated three L-749As (cns 2661, 2641 and 2640), registrations being CX-BBM, CX-BBN and CX-BCS. Lineas Aereas de Panama SA ordered four L-049S (cns 1968, 1965, 1967, 1962), the alloted registrations being RX-121, RX-123 and RX-124, of which RX-123 was not delivered and cn.1962 was used for spares. LAPSA (Lloyd Aero Paraguayo SA) owned an L-049, ZP-CAS (cn.1964), from December 1963, but it crashed the following month and had to be abandoned. RIPSA (Rutas Internacionales Pemanas SA) of Lima, Peru, ordered two L-749As but only operated one, OB-R-833 (cn.2610), an option on the second machine (cn.2522) was not taken up. Rymar, of Montevideo, Uruguay, flew an L-049 (cn.2071) during 1965, registered 86533. Lima-based Trans-Peruana de Aviacion SA operated four L-749s between 1967 and 1970 (cns 2544, 2557, 2564, 2645), registered OB-R-914, OB-R-915, OB-R-916 and OB-R-917. TRADO (Transporte Aereo Dominicano SA), of the Dominican Republic, flew two Constellations during 1979 and 1980, the first was an L-049 (cn.2070), HI-260, the second was an L-749A (cn.2522), HI-332. A third machine, another L-049 (cn.2085), was actually purchased and registered HI-270, but was used only for spares. In Chile a single Model L-049 (cn.2069), CAA was operated by Transportes Aereos Squella.

Until 1962 this L-1048H Super Connie was with Trans-Canada Airlines as CF-TEY (fleet No 413). In 1966 it served as a special tour aircraft for the Cincinnati Symphony Orchestra registered N9714C, then passed to Trans International Airlines Inc. as N9752C, before being sold to Central American Airways as shown in this 1978 picture.

This L-1049G Super 'G' Constellation is as delivered from Burbank to VARIG of Brazil. Registered PP-VDA, it had wingtip tanks fitted later with the logo 'Super G' painted on them.

By the late 1970s most of the early generation Lockheed Constellations (L-049 to L-749A series) had ended their careers, even in Latin American countries. It is believed the last of the type to be withdrawn from actual airline service was the L-749A HI-393 (cn.2603), which flew with the Dominican Republic airline Aerolineas Argo SA (Argo SA) until grounded, when the company ran into financial difficulties. This particular Constellation was in perfect airworthy condition when it was impounded at Santa Dominga.

During 1983 two L-749A Constellations, C-GXKO and C-GXKR (cns 2601 and 2604), were still operational in Canada, with Conifair Aviation Inc. These machines were used on anti-budworm spraying contracts, which entailed fifty hours of flying per annum, over the two month period when the budworm menace to trees was rife. The remainder of the year was usually spent under wraps at their base near Montreal.

Meanwhile, in the US, although TWA and Pan Am were regarded as having been the primary users of early Constellations, the type was quite widely employed on other American airlines. For example, Capitol International Airways Inc., which Jesse Starling and a partner started in 1946, as an aircraft sales, service and maintenance company at Nashville, Tennessee. After his partner left, Jesse Starling began a charter service as Capitol Airways, with a single war-surplus aircraft. This service grew steadily into an important American charter company, undertaking an appreciable amount of military contract work. At first, aircraft types such as ex-USAF Curriss C-46

Out to grass and looking rather forlorn is L-749A Constellation, N611 AS, at Mesa, USA, on 13 October 1978. An ex-ARGO S.A. machine (HI-393), it later operated with Aircraft Specialists Inc. on crop spraying and anti-fire borate bombing missions.

Commando transports and Douglas DC-4s were used. Soon an expanding network of domestic routes, especially in the eastern states of the US and the Great Lakes area, required more sophisticated aircraft and Capitol invested in a number of Lockheed Constellations, including twelve L-049s, seven L-749s and three L-049s, as reserve machines. In 1957 four L-749As were added to the Capitol fleet (cns 2663, 2671, 2566, 2504), registered as N4900C, N4901C, N4902C and N9816F. Later, Capitol had eleven Lockheed L-1049A Super Constellations in its fleet, these being registered, N1006C, N1007C, N1008C, N4715G, N4903C, N5401V, N5402V, N5403V, N5404V, N9718C and N9720C. On 1 June 1961, Capitol was taken over by United Airlines, completing the biggest airline merger up until that time.

In the period 1946-1950, American Overseas Airlines Inc. (AOA), later taken over by Pan Am, operated seven Model L-049 Constellations: N90921, N90922, N90923, N90924, N90925, N90926 and N90927. American Flyers Airline Corp. (which merged with Universal Airlines in 1971), flew four L-049s, previously operated by AOA. These were N88855, N88868, N90923 and N90925. Another three L-049s, operated by Miami-based ASA International Airlines from 1962 to 1963, were registered N86503, N86506 and N90926. Also based in Miami was Associated Air Transport Inc., which flew four Model L-749A Constellations during approximately the same period, registered as N101A, N103A, N117A and N120A. Braniff International

This L-1049G Super Connie had a chequered career, starting with QANTAS as VH-EAB in the 1960s. A decade later it went to Galaxy Trading Corp. (USA) as N93164, then to Atlantic Airways of Miami (N442LM), before passing to TABSA/Bolivian Airways of La Paz, followed by Lanzair (C.I.) Ltd of Jersey, Channel Islands (leased) and finally to Lance W Dreyer (USA). It is seen here as N11 SR at Brussels International Airport.

An L-749A registered to Royal Air Maroc as CN-CCP. This aircraft was later sold to COPISA, of Lima, Peru.

Another much-travelled Connie was this L-749A, originally acquired by Air India as VT-CQS, then to Australia as VH-EAF before acquisition by BOAC as G-ANTF Berkeley in September 1954. It was sold to Transocean Airlines in March 1958 as N9816F. By 1964 it was back in the UK with Ace Freighters as G-ANTF.

Airways, of Dallas, Texas, used two L-049s, N2520B and N 2521B, in the 1950s, while Californian Hawaiian Airlines flew one L-049, N74192, and four L-749A Constellations, registered N102A, N104A, N115A and N117A.

The Model L-749A Constellation proved to be popular among companies involved in fire-fighting and pesticide spraying contracts. Two such companies in the US were Aircraft Specialities Inc. (later Globair Inc.) and Christier Flying Services Inc. The first company, as well as owning a fleet of Super Constellations, flew two L-749As, N608AS and N611AS, while Christier operated five L-749As: N9463; N9464; N9465; N9466 and N9467.

Coastal Air Lines Inc., an American company, operated a small passenger-carrying fleet from 1958 until *c*.1962. Among their aircraft were four L-049 Constellations, registered N2737A, N2740A, N67953 and N86532. During the period 1961-1962, eight L-749A Constellations were employed by Great Lakes Airlines Inc., which flew them over its various routes, their registrations were, N1O2A, N104A, N105A, N106A, N107A, N109A, N115A and N117A. The Hughes Tool Co., one of Howard Hughes' companies, operated four Constellations, three L-049s (NC25600, N6000C, N6025C) and one L-749A (N6025C).

From the late 1940s until the 1970s numerous small and independent airlines operated Lockheed Constellations. Imperial Airlines Inc., which in 1961 flew three L-049s, N2737A, N67953 and N86532. Intercontinental Airways flew four L-049s, NC38936, NC90827, NC90828 (later NC67930) and NC90829, from 1951 to 1953. Lloyd Airlines Inc. had two Miami-based L-049s during 1961, N2520B and N2521B. Also operating out of Miami were four L-749A Constellations owned by Miami Airlines Inc., these were N5595A, N5596A, N9812F and N9813F. Another Miami-based company, Magic City Airways, flew two L-049s, N2521B and N86532. From 1964 until 1970, McCulloch International Airlines Inc., operated five Lockheed L-049s, registered N54214, N6000C, N90823, N90831 and N9412H. Among their small fleet of Lockheed aircraft, Modem Air Transport Inc., operating out of Miami and Trenton, New Jersey, had five L-049s, N2739A, N2741A, N67952, N86531 and 86533, as well as one L-749A, N103A.

An appreciable number of early generation Constellations were based in California. Examples include Trans California Airlines, which in the mid-1960s flew six L-749As, N102A, N104A, N105A, N106A, N107A and N115A, while from Oakland, Transocean Airlines operated four L-749As, N9812F, N9813F, N9816F and N9830F. From 1968 to 1970, Pacific Air Transport Inc. used two Constellations on its services. One was an L-049, N90816, and the other was an L-749A, N105A. Paradise Airlines, operating out of Burbank, employed three L-049s, N86504, N86506 and N9414H. Also at Burbank, during 1961-1962, was Paramount Airlines, operating three L-749As, N102A, N105A and N115A. Another Burbank-based company was Schwimmer Aviation, which flew three L-049s from 1948 until 1967. This trio were NC90827, NC90828 and NC90829. A fourth machine (cn.1962) had been purchased solely for spare parts. In California also, Standard Airways Inc., of

An early Connie variant, this British registered L-049, G-AMUP, is with Falcon Airlines in 1961. It was originally with BOAC and named Boston.

In its element is an L-749A Constellation, G-ALAL, of Ace Freighters. An ex-BOAC and Skyways machine, it was acquired by Ace Freighters together with two others from the same source, plus another four from South African Airways, all based at Gatwick in 1964. Later G-ALAL was sold to an operator in Puerto Rico, West Indies.

San Diego, operated a fleet of eight Constellations from 1960 until 1964. These were three L-049s, N6000C, N86517 and N90831, and five L-749As, N101A, N113A, N114A, N117A and N 120A.

The Constellation was also popular further north in the US. Six of the model 649A, N86521, N86522, N86523, N86524, N86525 and N86535, were operated by Chicago and Southern Airlines between 1950 and 1953. Later, during 1964, Dellair Inc. flew three L-049s, N6000C, N86517 and N90831. Other US users of L-049s included: Edde Airlines Inc., who flew N90816 and N9412H; Futura Airlines Inc., who flew N86504 and N 94144; Hawthorne Nevada Airlines, who used N9412H; Las Vegas Hacienda Inc., using N6000C, N90831 and N9409H; World Wide Airlines Inc., flying N6000C, N86517, N90831 and N9412H; Trans American Aeronautical Corp., who used N2520B, N2521B and N86532; International Caribbean Corp., who flew N86533; Trans International Airlines Inc. using N74192; US Airlines Inc. used N74192, which was leased from International Airlines Inc. from 1951-1952; Produce Custom Air Freight, who flew N9412H; Full Gospel Native Missionary Inc., users of N6000C and N90823; and John Ellis, who owned N86517, in the period 1967-1968.

Another shot of G-ALAL, this time in the early 1960s, when it is seen in the service of Skyways, London.

An L-1049C Super Connie when operating with Air Ceylon in 1959. Registered 4R-ACH, it was leased from KLM (ex-PH-LKA), but later went to Iberia of Spain as EC-AQL.

11 Effect of the Jet Age on Super Constellations and Starliners

At the beginning of the 1980s around a dozen Lockheed Constellations and Super Constellations remained in airline service, mostly in South America. The decline in operational status of this magnificent four-engine transport had been a slow process, starting in the late 1950s, with the introduction of the big jetliners, like the Boeing 707 and Douglas DC-8, into major airline service. As a consequence, the large airlines began selling off their surplus piston-engine types, such as the Douglas DC-4, 6 and 7 series, and numerous variants of the Lockheed Constellation and Super Constellation, which subsequently became readily available to secondary airline operators around the world.

Many Super Constellations, like the early generation Constellations before them, were acquired, for both passenger-carrying and freight-carrying, in Latin America. A prime example is AVIANCA, of Colombia, which purchased four Super Constellations to add to their six L-749As. Three of the Super Constellations were L-1049Cs, registered HK-175, HK-176 and HK-177. The fourth machine was an L-1049G, HK-184. These were used on the airline's transatlantic service to the European cities of Lisbon, Madrid, Paris and Rome, with later extensions to Hamburg and Frankfurt. On 1 June 1957, AVIANCA inaugurated a South American transcontinental flight to Lima, Peru. Meanwhile, the Cuban airline Cubana had started operating an L-1049C, CU-P-573, on 22 November 1954, on its Madrid and Mexico City routes. This aircraft was later supplemented by three Super-Gs, CU-T-601, CUT-602 and CUT-631, which started a daily, non-stop service between Havana and New York on 12 May 1956. One of these Super-Gs was normally leased to Chile's airline, Sociedad de Transportes Aereos Ltda (ALA), when its L-049 was undergoing overhaul.

Aerovias Guest, the Mexican airline, with a controlling purchased on 20 February 1959 by the Scandinavian Airline System (SAS), possessed a fleet of Lockheed L-749A Constellations to which it added three Super-Gs. These L-1049Gs, registered XA-NAC, XA-NAD and XA-NAF, were employed on the airline's Atlantic, Central American, Caribbean and Miami services.

In Venezuela, Linea Aeropostal Venezolana (LAV) had introduced a service to New York, using Constellations, on 12 March 1947. Between 1954 and 1956 they added eight Super Constellations to its fleet. These were two L-1049Es, YV-C-AMR, named *Rafael Urdaneia*, later re-registered as AMS, and YV-C-AMT, *Simon Bolivar*, later rebuilt as an L-1049G and re-registered YV-C-ANF, and six L-1049Gs registered YV-C-AME, YV-C-AMI, YV-C-ANB, YV-C-ANC, YV-C-AND and YV-C-ANE. In Brazil, the airline Redes Estaduais Aereas Limitada (REAL) acquired three of the convertible passenger and/or cargo L-1049H

Another Falcon Airways Constellation (G-AHEJ), an L-049, in 1961, having earlier operated with BOAC.

Super Constellations during February 1958. This trio later inaugurated a new service by REAL, to Los Angeles, via Manaus, Bogota and Mexico City. When another L-1049H joined the fleet, the service was extended, on 9 July 1960, to include a transpacific route to Tokyo, calling at Honolulu. These four L-1049Hs, which later went to VARIG of Brazil, were registered PP-YSA, PP-YSB, PP-YSC and PP-YSD, the same registrations applying to both airlines.

In February 1953, VARIG (Empresa de Viacao Aerea Rio Grandense SA) was advised by the Brazilian Government that it could operate a new service from Brazil to New York. Consequently, an immediate order was placed with Lockheed for three L-1049E Super Constellations, which were allotted registrations PP-VDA, PP-VDB and PP-VDC. This contract was changed to one for three of the newer L-1049G Super-Gs then becoming available. The same registrations intended for the L-1049Es were applied to the Super-G Constellations which, after arriving at Rio de Janeiro, inaugurated VARIG's service to New York, via Belem, Port of Spain and Ciudad Trujillo, (Dominican Republic) on 2 August 1955. The following November VARIG extended its route mileage by commencing a service to Buenos Aires, at the same time acquiring three more L-1049Gs, PP-VDD, PP-VDE and PP-VDF, in addition to the four L-1049Hs bought from REAL, mentioned previously.

Numerous other Latin American operators flew Super Constellations, which include a number which will now be briefly described. Aeromar Dominican Republic leased an L-1049H, N1007C, from Air Cargo Support from 1977 to 1979. Aerotours Dominicano, flew an L-1049, HI-228, and an L-1049C, HI-329, from

1974 to 1979. Aerotransportes Entre Rios SRL, of Argentina, used an L-1049G, LV-IXZ, and three L-1049Hs, LV-PJU (later JHF), LV-PJ10 and LV-PKW (later JJO). Aerovias Panama, used two L-1049Gs, HP-280 and HP-281. AFISA, of Panama, flew the L-1049H, N6917C (later HP-526).

Aviateca, of Guatemala, used an L-1049H, N6392C. Bolivian International Airways used an L-1049H, CP-998. CAUSA, of Uruguay,flew L-1049H, CX-BEM. LEBCA, of Venezuela, flew two L-1049Hs, YV-C-LBI and YV-C-LBP. Lineas Aereas Patagonias Argentinas SRL, used an L-1049H, LV-ILW. RAPSA, of Panama, used an ex-TWA L-1049C, HP-475, and an L-1049G, HP-467. TABSA, of Bolivia, used two L-1049Hs, cns 4801 and 4807, but both with same CP-797 registration, and also operated L-1049G (cn.4581), known to have been N442LM at one time. Transcontinental SA, of Argentina, which commenced a Buenos Aires to New York service in September 1958 using L-1049Hs LV-FTU and LV-FTV. VIASA, of Venezuela, which in 1961 was operating one L-1049E, YV-C-ANF, and two Super-Gs, YC-C-AME and YC-C-AMI.

Super Constellations made redundant by major airlines as the big jetliners moved in were soon snapped up by numerous companies, from those running a substantial fleet of aircraft down to one-plane operators. In the US alone, more than sixty companies became Super Constellation operators and at one time exceeded those operating the type in Latin American countries. Many second-hand Super Constellations were sold to secondary airlines in the

Miami International Airport, March 1978. A Lockheed L-1049C Super Constellation, registration N6224C, which at one time operated with Eastern Air Lines, fleet number 224.

Seen here during 1971, this L-1049G Super Connie (N45516) is with the North Slope Supply Co., of Anchorage, Alaska. An ex-Flying Tigers machine, it was at one time with KLM (PH-LKL), then Lance W. Dreyer. It later passed to Aircraft Specialities Inc. (later Globair), with whom it flew on crop spraying and anti-fire borate bombing duties, at least into the early 1980s.

An L-1049C, N6227C, at Miami International Airport in March 1978. It originally flew with Eastern Air Lines (fleet No 227), later going to Air Cargo Support in 1973. Eventually it went to Proimex International, of Denver, Colorado, from where it was allocated to Miami for spares.

Middle and Far East, Africa and New Zealand, where they operated in both passenger-carrying and freight-transport configurations.

European operators of the Super Constellation were fewer, by comparison, and can be considered in a little more detail. For example, Aer Lingus began its Dublin to New York service, on 28 April 1958, with an L-1049C, N 1005C, leased from SWA. This was joined later by a Super-G, N611C, and two L-1049Hs, N1008C and N1009C. These four Super Constellations flew with Aer Lingus until early 1961, when they were superseded by Boeing 707-048 jets.

As well as Air France, two other French concerns using Super Constellations were Air Fret and Catair. Both companies flew a mixed fleet of L-1049C and L-1049G Super Constellations. Air Fret's one L-1049C, F-BRAD, operated alongside the three Super Gs, F-BHBB, F-BHBI and F-BHML. All four were ex-Air France aircraft. Catair owned three L-1049Cs, F-BGNC, F-BGNH and F-BGNG, and two L-1049Gs, F-BHBE and F-BHMI. When necessary, they also used Air Fret's L-1049C. In additon, SAFA, of Paris, flew L-1049Gs chartered from Air France.

Lanzair (CI) Ltd, of Jersey, Channel Islands, flew a single leased L-1049G during the mid-1970s, which carried the registration N11SR. In Spain, Inter-City

One of three L-1049C Super Connies leased by Seaboard & Western Airlines to Aerlinte Eireann (later Aer Lingus) between 1958 and 1960, this machine registered N1005C, was named Brighid *and used on the airline's Dublin to New York service.*

This ex-Air France L-1049G super Connie (F-BHML) is seen here during 1970 after transferring to the French airline Compagnie Air Fret. During 1960 it was also chartered to Tunis Air.

Airways, of Madrid, flew a leased L-1049H, N469C, in 1968. Belgian airline, SABENA, leased three L-1049H Super Constellations, N1006C, N1007C and N1008C, from America's SWA.

In Portugal, Transportes Aereos Portugueses (TAP) received its first L-1049G, CS-TLA, on 15 July 1955. This aircraft was named *Vasco da Gama*. It entered service on TAP's European routes, together with those to Luanda and Lourenco Marques, Mozambique. This aircraft was subsequently joined by four additional L-1049Gs and one L-1049H, registered CS-TLB, CS-TLC, CS-TLE, CS-TLF and CS-TLD, respectively.

Meanwhile, PanAm were flying a non-stop, transatlantic service with Douglas DC-7s, which prompted TWA to persuade Lockheed to build the L-1649A Starliner, a direct development from the L-1049G, and a rival contender to PanAm on the Atlantic route. TWA introduced this ultimate Constellation variant on their New York London Paris service on 1 June 1957, naming their latest acquisition from Lockheed the Jetstream class. Although TWA purchased twenty-nine Starliners, the type did not last long in the company's service. The jet-era had already started and the death-knell for piston-engine airliners in major airline service was sounding loud and clear. In the event, at least twelve of those L-1649As acquired by TWA, were operated as freighters from 1960 onwards.

In Europe, Air France placed a contract with Lockheed for ten L-1649As, registered F-BHBK, F-BHBL, F-BHBM, F-BHBN, F-BHBO, F-BHBP, F-BHBQ, F-BHBR, F-BHBS and F-BHBT, while Lufthansa purchased four, registered D-ALUB, D-ALAN, D-ALER and D-ALOL. Two of Lufthansa's machines flew as freighters, and two, D-ALER and D-ALOL, flew with Condor Flugdienst, from 1960 to 1962. As this company was, at the time, a subsidiary of Lufthansa, the machines retained the same registrations. These latter two aircraft later passed to Trek Airways (Pty) Ltd, of South Africa, becoming ZS-DTM and ZS-DVJ. However, although still owned by Trek, this pair operated in the colours of Luxembourg's Luxair airline, from 1964 to 1969, as LX-LGZ and LX-LGX, and were joined by a third Luxair L-1649A Starliner, LX-LGY.

In the US, World Airways Inc. had added four L-1649As to their Super Constellation fleet. These Starliners were registered N4511, N4512, N4517 and N4520. N4517 and N4520 were the pair that flew with Lufthansa, Condor Flugdienst, Trek Airways (Pty) Ltd and Luxair. This was a good example of how the forty-three Starliners built changed hands, as indeed had the earlier series of Constellations and Super Constellations. One L-1649A was operated by a religious/political organization, known as the Moral Rearmament Organization, during 1964-1965. Registered N7314C, this aircraft had originally belonged to TWA. Another L-1649A, N974R, initially owned by World Airways, as N45512, operated as a freighter during 1976-1977, with Proimex International, of Denver, Colorado.

During the period 1968-1969, the Prudhoe Bay Oil Distributing Co. operated three L-1649As, N7315C, N7316C and N8083H, in pure cargo-carrying configuration, while Trans American Leasing Inc., of Miami, acquired three Starliners, N7311 C, N7322C and N7324C, for use between 1968 and 1973. The aforementioned N974R flew with CJS Aircargo from

Another ex-Air France L-049C Super Connie, F-BRAD, this time operating with the French airline CATAIR. Note the type of motorised access gangways.

An L-1649A Starliner of Trek Airways, South Africa, registration ZS-DVJ. Until 1964 this aircraft was with World Airways Inc, Oakland, California. It then passed to Lufthansa as D-ALOL, also flying with Condor, a subsidiary of Lufthansa, before being acquired by Trek Airways. This machine also flew under Luxair colours as LX-LGX.

1970 until 1972. The Hughes Tool Co. operated another L-1649A, N7310C. Lockheed themselves flew a Starliner (cn.1001), with three different registrations, N1649, N90968 and N 1102, applied over a period of time, these. During the mid-1960s an airline known as Starflite operated several L-1649A Starliners, but no other details of these are available at the time of writing. West-Air Inc., of Bethel, Alaska, owned five L-1649As of which three, N7316C, N8083H and N974R (the latter having changed hands again), were operational, and two, N7312C and N7315C, were held for spares. As well as N974R, it is noticeable that a number of aircraft exchanged hands on several occasions.

12. Constellation – End of the Flightpath

Many Lockheed Constellation variants continued operating in regular service with secondary airline companies until the late 1960s. In the US, Pacific Northern Airlines Inc. flew nine L-749A Constellations, N114A, N10401, N10403, N1593V, N6017C, N6022C, N86523, N86524 and N86525, from 1955 until 1967. However, like many of their contemporaries, Pacific Northern passed some of its Constellations on to other companies. Five went to Western Airlines Inc., of Los Angeles, in 1967. These machines were N1593V, N6017C, N6022C, N86524 and N86525. A sixth L-749A, N1552V, was added to the Western Airlines fleet later. Initially, N1552V, N1593V, N6017C and N6022C were allotted Western fleet numbers 52V, 93V, 17C and 22C, but these were eventually altered to 552, 593, 517 and 522, while the remaining N86524 and N86525 were similarly altered, becoming Western fleet numbers 524 and 525.

Two L-749As, N4902C and N9812F, operated with World Wide Airlines Inc. Wien Alaskan Airlines flew an L-749A, N7777G. Trans International Airlines Inc. owned another L-749A, N4901C, although this was normally leased out, as was another L-749A, N6012C, owned by Unlimited Leasing Inc. from 1970 until 1979. It is not certain whether or not an L-749A owned by Las Vegas Hacienda, N120A, was employed on scheduled services. An ex-Western Airlines L-749A, N1593V, was sold privately, to a Claude R. Soto, during 1969.

In the UK, during 1961, Falcon Airways Ltd had purchased three L-049 Constellations, registered G-AHEJ, G-AHEL and G-AMUP. In addition, the company acquired another L-049 for Austria's Aero-Transport, which received the registration OE-IFA. Elsewhere, several airlines continued operating L-749As on their scheduled routes, although some were employed purely as freighters, especially when the new Super Constellations began arriving. Some companies flew the Constellations only as freighters. One example is the British-based Ace Freighters Ltd, which from 1964 onwards operated eight L-749As, registered G-ALAK, G-ALAL, G-ANTF, G-ANUR, G-ASYF, G-ASYS, G-ASYT and G-ASYU.

Ireland's Aerlinte Ekeann (later Aer Lingus) had ordered five L-749A Constellations in 1947 for their intended transatlantic service to New York. These were all delivered on 30 September 1947 and registered EI-ACR, EI-ACS, EI-ADM, EI-ADD and EI-ADE. However, the transatlantic service was temporarily abandoned and, following a short period of use on the Dublin to UK and European routes, these five L-749As were sold to BOAC in June 1948. Also in Europe, Aero-Transport, of Austria, flew two L-749As, OE-IFE

Lockheed L-1649A Starliner, LX-LGZ, of Luxembourg's airline Luxair, stands in front of the old apron control tower at Gatwick on a very wet day in the late 1950s.

and OE-IFO, in addition to the aforementioned L-049, OE-IFA, from 1961 to 1964, while another L-049, ex-G-AHEJ, was used as a spares machine.

Four L-749A Constellations were flown by Air Algerie from 1955 to 1961, carrying the French registrations F-BAZE, F-BAZG, F-BBDV and F-BAZJ. Air Afrique operated one L-749A, French registered as F-BAZK (later becoming Moroccan registered as CN-CCM), from 1961 onwards. Air Ceylon had ordered two L-749As in 1956, but this order lapsed, although one L-749A, PH-LDP, was leased from Holland's KLM airline. In 1957 three more of KLM's L-749As, PH-LDS, PH-LDT and PH-LDK, were added to Air Ceylon's fleet. Three L-749As, registered F-BAZK, F-BAZL and F-BAZF, were operated by Air Inter of Paris from 1961 to 1962, having been leased from Air France. As mentioned previously, two L-749A 'tanker' Constellations operated well into the 1980s with Conifalr Aviation of Canada. These machines, C-GXKO and C-GXKR, had earlier flown with Beaver Air Spray, when a third L-749A, C-GXKS, accompanied them on similar operations.

In Africa, Britair East Africa Ltd, based in Kenya, flew an old Lockheed Model L-049, 5Y-ABF (ex-G-AHEL). In 1957 Ethiopian Airlines acquired an L-749A, ET-T-35, but, after entering service on 10 June, this aircraft crashed in July and was written off. Royal Air Burundi was formed in 1962 by a group of American businessmen. Their first aircraft was a Lockheed L-049 Constellation, with the registration N9412H. Royal Air Maroc (RAM), of Morocco, operated five Model L-749As between 1957 and 1970. The first aircraft, CN-CCR, arrived during October 1957. Three more, CC-CCP, CC-CCN and CC-CCO, arrived in 1960, and the fifth machine, CC-CCM arrived in 1962. From 1950 onwards, South African Airways (SAA) operated four L-749As, ZS-DBR, ZS-DBS, ZS-DBT and ZS-DBU. Two of these aircraft, ZS-DBS and ZS-DBU, later flew with with South Africa's Trek Airways (Pty) Ltd from 1961 to 1968. North Africa's Tunis Air operated an L-749A Constellation from 1961 onwards. This machine was chartered from Air France and registered F-BAZO.

A considerable number of early Constellations ended up as the sole representative of the type within some of the smaller airlines and companies, or were flown having been leased from a larger company. Some aircraft coming under this category and not already referred to include: an L-049 of Cubana, CU-T547, which was leased, from 1957 to 1959, to Sociedad de Transporte Aereos Ltd (ALA), of Chile, (later Cinta-Linea Aerea Chilena, finally absorbed by LADECO.).

Carib Airways Inc., US, flew an L-749A, N6021C, during 1979. In 1969-1970 another L-749A, N6017C, was owned by Vincent M. Castora. This aircraft was later impounded in Panama City. Starting in 1967, Central American Airways Flying Service Inc. operated an L-749A, N273R, for a number of years. CJS Cargo Inc., another American company, flew an L-749A, N7777G, from 1970 to 1972. Another L-749A, N9812F, owned by Miami Airlines, was leased during 1960 to Iceland's Loftleioir Creykjavik (Icelandic Airlines).

In 1972, SS&T Aerial Contracting, of Arizona, US, a company concerned with anti-pest borate-bombing, purchased a Lockheed L-049 Constellation, N90816, for this purpose. It is believed this machine was never used and, after about five years in storage, it was sold (buyer not known). Another L-749A,

A 1961 shot of an early L-049 Constellation, G-AHEL, belonging to Falcon Airways. This machine was originally with BOAC.

CP-797, was purchased in 1968 by Trans Bolivian Airlines, of La Paz, but, according to records, it too was not used. Luxembourg-based Interocean Airways SA had operated one L-749A, LX-1 OK, during 1964. Some years earlier, between 1961 and 1962, British-based Trans-European Airways flew L-049, G-AHEL, having ordered a second L-049 Constellation, G-AHRK, which was not delivered, although two other L-049s, G-AHEJ and G-AMUP, were used for spares.

The UK was the last European stronghold of the early Constellations in the mid-1960s, where Skyways of London Ltd operated one L-149, G-ARXE, and four L-749As, G-ALAK, G-ALAL, G-ANUP and G-ANUR. These five Constellations were used mainly on freight services to the Far East, as part of a contract for BOAC. Some of the last L-749As in American service also operated in the freighting role. Four of the type formed part of a cargo fleet, which included a number of Super Constellations, owned by Lance W. Dreyer, which incorporated Transitional Cargo Inc., UNUM Inc., Air Cargo International Inc. and Air International Inc. This group's four L-749As were

Three Lockheed L-749A Constellations awaiting delivery to Aerlinte Eireann in 1947. Intended for the Irish airline's trans-Atlantic route, this plan was postponed indefinitely and these aircraft along with two others were sold to BOAC in June 1948.

Close-up view of empennage arrangement on an Air France L-049 Connie with two other identical aircraft in the background, plus a couple of Douglas DC-6Bs in the distance.

N1206, N6021C, N7777G and N86524 (some of these machines had changed hands several times before and are referred to elsewhere in this book).

Despite the appearance of more advanced types of aircraft by 1960, a suprising number of early Constellations still remained in service with some of the world's principal airlines. These included: Air France, with fifteen; Braniff, with two; Capital Airlines, with eleven; Cubana, with one; El-A1, with one; KLM, with ten; Pacific Northern, with six; Panair do Brasil, with twelve; South African Airways, with four and Transocean, with one. TWA was still operating quite a number of its vast Constellation fleet at that time. At one time the airline owned forty-two L-049s, twelve L-749s, twenty-nine L-749As and the six C-69s which it flew as part of the USAAF Air Transport Command system.

One of the finest Constellations extant in Europe belongs to the Science Museum and is housed in their site at Wroughton, Wiltshire, UK. This machine is an L-749 which had a very chequered career. It went to KLM in 1947, as PH-TET (later PH-LDT), flying KLM's routes to Australia, Japan, South Africa and the US, until 1960, when it was replaced by the airline's

Derelict and minus its engines, this L-749A Constellation was withdrawn from use in 1966 after serving as G-ASYT with Ace Freighters. Prior to that it had flown with South African Airways as ZS-DBT.

new Douglas DC-8 jet transport and put into storage. Some three years later it was sold to Wein Alaskan Airlines, converted to a mixed passenger/cargo configuration and allotted the US registration N7777G. From 1964 until 1966 it operated from Fairbanks, Alaska, before passing to several US-based companies, including Lance W. Dreyer and CJS Aircargo Inc. In 1973 N7777G went to Lanzair (CI) Ltd, of Jersey, Channel Islands, where it flew with the company's other Constellation, an L-749A, N273R. The same year N7777G accompanied the rock group, the Rolling Stones, on their Far East tour. In 1974 it flew a service ferrying cattle between Ireland and Libya but after only one trip N7777G remained at Dublin airport, out of use and derelict. In 1982 it was rescued by a concern known as Aces High. Thanks to Mike Woodley, the managing director of Aces High, the seven year fee for 'parking' at Dublin airport was attended to, and it was decided to restore N7777G to an airworthy condition, before flying it to England. This plan was abandoned, however, and the old Constellation had to be dismantled and taken by road to Dublin Docks, for passage to Fleetwood, UK, aboard the B&I Line vessel *Tipperary*. Initially registered G-CONI, this L-749 was eventually donated to the Science Museum's Air Transport collection at Wroughton, where it was restored and repainted in an original American colour scheme, as a Constellation of TWA *c.*1950-1955, and given its original registration of N7777G. It has become one of the star attractions on public open days at Wroughton.

Pictured at Miami International Airport in March 1978, this L-749A Connie, N6021 C, was originally with TWA (fleet No 821). It later flew with Unlimited Leasing Inc (USA), Lance W Dreyer and Carib Airways Inc. of Miami.

The *Musee de l'Air*, in Paris, houses another well-displayed Lockheed L-749 Constellation (cn.2503), which originally flew with Pan Am as N86520, named *Clipper America*. It then went to Aerovias Guest as XA-GOQ. It was returned to Lockheed in 1948, before going to Air France in 1949 as F-BAZU. After its service with Air France it was stored at Paris-Orly, until 1963, when it went to the *Centre d'Essals*. Allotted the civil registration F-ZVMV, it was used as an engine test-bed for a time, with the power-plant on test mounted above the fuselage on a sturdy two-legged pylon. It was in a military finish at the time, with usual national markings, despite the civil registration. This machine was later donated to the *Musee de l'Air*.

Thus, on both sides of the Channel fine examples of a Lockheed Model L-749 Constellation exist. These aircraft are representative of a type which did much to revolutionize world air travel after the Second World War. A class of aeroplane that provided reliable, speedy and comparatively comfortable service to many of the world's leading airlines, until superseded by more modern types, which included the Super Constellation and the Starliner. The latter, became the last in a line of magnificent four-engine airliners manufactured by Lockheed. Although most Starliners had been withdrawn from the fleets of primary users by the 1960s, some of the original old Constellations plodded on for a number of years around Latin America into the 1970s, a fitting tribute to what has come to be regarded as a classic among the world's greatest civil aircraft.

Derelict at Kingman in November 1976, a very unbalanced L-1049H Super Connie reflects on its long career with Flying Tiger Line Inc (fleet No 819), KLM (as PH-LKN), World Airways Inc, of Oakland, California, Lance W Dreyer Inc,. North Slope Supply Company Inc., of Anchorage, Alaska, Aircraft Specialities Inc. (later Globair Inc.), which operated crop spraying and borate bombing duties. The registration N45515 is still quite visible on the rear fuselage.

Lockheed L-749A Constellation, N7777G, at Dublin Airport on 16 April 1979. Originally with KLM in 1947 as PH-TET (later PH-LDT), it was sold and put into storage for three years before conversion to a mixed passenger and freight configuration, then moved to Wien Alaska Airlines as N7777G in 1964. It was sold again in 1966 and used by a number of companies until 1974 and then held disused at Dublin until, in March 1982, it was bought by 'Aces High' and acquired by the Science Museum in 1983 to be displayed in TWA colours at Wroughton.

Appendix 1
Technical Data

Model C-69:
This was the original military transport version of 1943.

Power-plant:	four 2,200hp Wright R-3350-35, 18-cylinder Wright Cyclone air-cooled radial engines driving 3-blade Hamilton Standard Hydromatic full-leathering propellers.
Performance:	maximum speed, 347mph at 20,000ft; cruising speed, 275mph; landing speed, 77mph; climb, 1,620ft per minute; range (normal), 2,400 miles; service ceiling, 25,300ft.
Weights:	empty, 50,000lb; loaded (maximum take-off), 72,000lb.
Dimensions:	span, 123ft; length, 95ft 2in; height, 23ft 8in; wing area, 1,650sq. ft.

Model L-049:
Basically, this was a USAAF C-69 conversion, with an increase in maximum take-off weight to 86,250lb and modified Wright engines, 2,200hp 745C18BA3s instead of the BA1s.

Model L-049A:
As the L-049, but with reinforced front wing spar and main landing gear side-struts. Maximum take-off weight increased to 90,000lb.

Model L-049B:
As the L-049A, but with an increased maximum take-off weight of 93,000lb. It incorporated fuselage external rails and new metering pins were fitted in the main landing gear.

Model L-049C:
As the L-049B, but with an MLG drag strut damper and a 15:1 boost ratio included.

Model L-049D:
As the L-049C, but with reinforced inner wing and an increase in maximum take-off weight to 96,000lb.

Model L-149:
As the L-049D, but it incorporated fuel tanks in modified outer wing panels, and maximum take-off weight was increased to 100,000lb.

Model L-649

A new version featuring uprated 2,500hp Wright 749C 18BD1 engines, revised engine cowlings (range-peel type) and installation of air-conditioning. It was much the same as the L-049B, but with an MLG drag strut damper and a 15:1 elevator boost, improved furnishings and shock-mounting cabin walls (this was the first, true, civil Constellation). Maximum take-off weight was 94,000lb.

Model L-649A:

As the L-649, but containing reinforcements to the fuselage and inner wing, modified brakes and an increase to the maximum take-off weight to 98,000lb.

Model L-749:

Similar to the L-649A, but with modified outer wing panels, containing extra fuel tanks, and an increase in maximum take-off weight to 102,000lb.

Model L-749A:

As the L-749, but it incorporated strengthening of the fuselage, inner wing and main landing gear. It also had a modified braking system and an increase in maximum take-off weight to 107,000lb.

Model L-1049:

A new variant, known as the Super Constellation. The fuselage length was increased by 18.4ft. It was pressurized from 8,000 to 25,000ft and incorporated: a new style of windscreen; redesigned cabin windows of rectangular shape; optional centre-section fuel tanks; four 2,700hp Wright 975C118CB1 (R-3350-CA1) Cyclone radial engines. It had a maximum take-off weight of 120,000lb.

Model L-1049A:

This was a new military version, designated R7V-1, R7V-2, WV-1 and WV-2, for the US Navy, and C-121A, VC-121B, RC-121C and RC-121D, for the US Air Force.

Model L-1049B:

A civil freighter version, based on the military L-1049A, with 3,250hp, Wright 972TC18DA1 (R-3350-DA1) Turbo-Compound radial engines and a strengthened airframe to allow a maximum take-off weight of 130,000lb. Seaboard and Western ordered four L-1049Bs but this order was cancelled in favour of the updated Model L-1049D.

Model L-1049C:

This was the first passenger-carrying version powered by Turbo Compound engines. It was fitted with a Dreyfuss-styled interior. Its maximum take-off weight increased to 133,000lb.

Model L-1049D:

As the L-1049C, but with modified wing and fuselage to allow for a maximum take-off weight of 150,000lb. As a pure freighter version it had a heavy-duty floor and cargo doors fitted.

Model L-1049E:

As the L-1049C, but modified to have up to 150,000lb maximum take-off weight capability. Of twenty-six built, a large proportion were converted to L-1049G standard while still on the production line.

Model L-1049F:

This was a Lockheed designation for the military C-121C version, of which thirty-three were completed.

Model L-1049G:

The most successful and prolific of the L-1049 series, which warrants a more detailed summary of data. It was an update of the L-1049E, with Wright TC-18-DA3 Turbo-Compound radial engines. It featured wing-tip tanks, which increased total fuel capacity to 6,453 gallons (Imperial).

Performance:	maximum speed, 362mph; cruising speed (normal at 20,000ft), 305mph; climb (gross weight at sea level), 1,140ft per minute; landing speed, 99.5mph; range (in still air with maximum fuel, with full reserves), 5,100 miles, or normal range (maximum fuel with no reserves), 4,820 miles at 10,000ft; service ceiling, 27,600ft.
Weight:	empty (equipped), 79,000lb; loaded (maximum take-off), 141,700lb.
Dimensions:	span, 123ft (126ft 2in. over the tip tanks); length 113ft 7in. (116ft 2in. with radar nose); height, 24ft 9in; wing area, 1,650sq.ft.

Model L-1249 (R7V-2):

A turboprop development based on the L-1049D. It was powered by four Pratt & Whitney T-34 turboprop engines.

Models L-1249A, 1249B, 1449 and 1549:

All these were Lockheed projects only.

Model L-1049H:

A dual-purpose convertible version of the L-1049G, for use as a passenger and/or freighter aircraft. It was fitted with heavy duty flooring and freight doors, as with the L-1049D. It had uprated 3,400hp TC-18-EA-6 Turbo Compound engines could be fitted, resulting in a 140,000lb maximum take-off weight. This was final version of Super Constellation, the last being delivered in November 1958.

Model L-1649A Starliner:

This was a production version of an extra-long-range transport. Basically, it was an L-1049G fuselage married to a newly-designed wing incorporating laminar flow and increased span, which contained additional fuel. It was powered by four 3,400hp Wright R-3350-988TC-18EA-2 Turbo Compound radial engines, driving three-blade, Hamilton Standard Hydromatic propellers featuring reverse pitch.

Performance: maximum speed, 377mph at 18,600ft; cruising speed (normal), 290mph at 22,000ft.

Weights: empty, 91,645lb; loaded (maximum take-off), 160,000lb.

Dimensions: span, 150ft; length (with radar nose), 116ft 2in; height, 24ft 9in; wing area, 1,850 sq.ft.

Appendix 2
Major Airline Service

Trans World Airways (TWA)

C-69: (Under jurisdiction of USAAF Air Transport Command) six from 1944.

L-049: (Including military conversions from fourteen machines delivered to the USAAF, or on the production line on VJ Day, after which military orders were cancelled) forty-two entered service, two of which, NX54212 and NX54214 (cns 1971 and 1974), were employed on pilot training only.

L-749: Twelve entered service.

L-749A: Of twenty-eight which entered service at least five, N6010C, N6012C, N6013C, N86521 and N86522 (cns 2646, 2648, 2649, 2642 and 2653), were produced in sleeper configuration for night services.

L-1049: Ten entered service.

L-1049C: Only seven are believed to have entered service. As far as is known cns were 4550, 4551, 4552, 4554, 4555, 4556 and 4557.

L-1049G: Twenty-nine were delivered.

L-1049H: Nine entered service.

L-1649A: Deliveries totalled twenty-nine, but of these at least twelve operated in freighter configuration from 1960-1961.

Air France

L-049: At least four were acquired for service in 1947.

L-749: A total of fourteen entered service.

L-749A: Ten were acquired.

L-1049C: Ten entered service.

L-1049G: Fourteen were purchased.

L-1649A: Ten flew in Air France service.

British Overseas Airways Corporation (BOAC)

L-049:   Eight entered service.

L-749:   Five were delivered.

L-749A: Twelve entered service between 1953 and 1955.

Eastern Air lines Inc

L-049:   Twelve were taken on charge.

L-649:   Fourteen were delivered.

L-749:   Seven were acquired.

L-1049:   Fourteen were acquired.

L-1049C: Seventeen were delivered.

L-1049G: Ten entered service.

L-1049H: Five were put into service.

Flying Tiger Line Inc

L-1049H: Twenty-one were purchased.

KLM (Royal Dutch Airlines)

L-049:   Six were delivered.

L-749:   Thirteen entered service.

L-749A: Seven were acquired.

L-1049C: Thirteen were delivered.

L-1049G: Six were purchased.

L-1049H: Three entered service.

Lufthansa

L-1049G: Eight were delivered.

L-1049H: Two entered service.

L-1649A: Four entered service.

Pan American World Airways

C-69:   (Under jurisdiction of USAAF Air Transport Command) one in 1945.

L-049:   Twenty-nine were delivered, one was sent directly to Panair do Brasil.

L-749:   One was delivered and put into service.

L-749A: Only one entered service.

L-1049:   Just one entered service.

Panair do Brasil

L-049:   Eleven.

L-149:   Five were received.

QANTAS

L-749:   Took delivery of six, and flew one leased machine.

L-1049C: Operated four.

L-1049G: Took delivery of ten.

L-1049H: Two were received.

Trans Canada Air Lines Inc

L-1049C: Operated five.

L-1049E: Flew three.

L-1049G: Flew four.

L-1049H: Only two entered service.

Air India International

L-749:   Took delivery of three.

L-749A: Four entered service.

L-1049C: Two entered service.

L-1049E: Three entered service.

L-1049G: Five entered service.